BUSINESS, TECHNOLOGY AND FINANCE

ASSET MANAGEMENT FIRMS, FINANCIAL STABILITY AND THE FSOC

ELEMENTS AND CONSIDERATIONS

BUSINESS, TECHNOLOGY AND FINANCE

Additional books in this series can be found on Nova's website under the Series tab.

Additional e-books in this series can be found on Nova's website under the e-book tab.

BUSINESS, TECHNOLOGY AND FINANCE

ASSET MANAGEMENT FIRMS, FINANCIAL STABILITY AND THE FSOC

ELEMENTS AND CONSIDERATIONS

LEAH T. MCLAIN
EDITOR

NOVINKA

New York

For permission to use material from this book please contact us:
Telephone 631-231-7269; Fax 631-231-8175
Web Site: http://www.novapublishers.com

Library of Congress Cataloging-in-Publication Data

ISBN: 978-1-63117-722-4

Published by Nova Science Publishers, Inc. † New York

CONTENTS

Preface		**vii**
Chapter 1	Asset Management and Financial Stability *Office of Financial Research*	**1**
Chapter 2	Financial Stability Oversight Council: A Framework to Mitigate Systemic Risk *Edward V. Murphy*	**43**
Chapter 3	Monitoring the Financial System *Ben S. Bernanke*	**79**
Index		**91**

PREFACE

Asset managers provide investment management services and ancillary services to clients as fiduciary agents. The diversity of clients' needs results in a wide variety of firm structures and business models, ranging from investment boutiques that focus on a single product or clientele to large, complex financial institutions that offer multiple services. This book provides a brief overview of the asset management industry and an analysis of how asset management firms and the activities in which they engage can introduce vulnerabilities that could pose, amplify, or transmit threats to financial stability. It also describes the mission, membership, and scope of the Financial Stability Oversight Council (FSOC), which was created as part of a comprehensive reform of banking and securities market regulators. It provides an analysis of several major policy issues related to the FSOC that may come before the 113th Congress.

Chapter 1 – This is a report issued by the Office of Financial Research, U.S. Department of the Treasury, Asset Management and Financial Stability, on dated September 2013.

Chapter 2 – This is a Report of Congressional Research Service prepared for Members and Committees of Congress, on Financial Stability Oversight Council: A Framework to Mitigate Systemic Risk, dated May 21, 2013.

Chapter 3 – This is a speech by the Chairman of the Federal Reserve Board, on Monitoring the Financial System, presented at the 49th Annual Conference on Bank Structure and Competition sponsored by the Federal Reserve Bank of Chicago, May 10, 2013.

In: Asset Management ...
Editor: Leah T. McLain

ISBN: 978-1-63117-722-4

Chapter 1

ASSET MANAGEMENT AND FINANCIAL STABILITY*

Office of Financial Research

INTRODUCTION

This report provides a brief overview of the asset management industry and an analysis of how asset management firms and the activities in which they engage can introduce vulnerabilities that could pose, amplify, or transmit threats to financial stability.

The Financial Stability Oversight Council (the Council) decided to study the activities of asset management firms to better inform its analysis of whether—and how—to consider such firms for enhanced prudential standards and supervision under Section 113 of the Dodd-Frank Act.[1] The Council asked the Office of Financial Research (OFR), in collaboration with Council members, to provide data and analysis to inform this consideration. This study responds to that request by analyzing industry activities, describing the factors that make the industry and individual firms vulnerable to financial shocks, and considering the channels through which the industry could transmit risks across financial markets.

The U.S. asset management industry oversees the allocation of approximately $53 trillion in financial assets (see Figure 1). The industry is

* This is an edited, reformatted and augmented version of a report issued by the Office of Financial Research, U.S. Department of the Treasury, dated September 2013.

central to the allocation of financial assets on behalf of investors. By facilitating investment for a broad cross-section of individuals and institutions, discretionary asset management plays a key role in capital formation and credit intermediation, while spreading any gains or losses across a diverse population of market participants. The industry is marked by a high degree of innovation, with new products and technologies frequently reshaping the competitive landscape and changing the way that financial services are provided.

Asset management firms and the funds that they manage transact with other financial institutions to transfer risks, achieve price discovery, and invest capital globally through a variety of activities. Asset management activities include allocating assets and selecting securities, using a variety of investment strategies in registered and non-registered funds; enhancing returns with derivatives or leverage; and creating customized investment solutions for larger clients, primarily through so-called separate accounts.

These activities differ in important ways from commercial banking and insurance activities. Asset managers act primarily as agents: managing assets on behalf of clients as opposed to investing on the managers' behalf. Losses are borne by—and gains accrue to—clients rather than asset management firms. In contrast, commercial banks and insurance companies typically act as principals: accepting deposits with a liability of redemption at par and on demand, or assuming specified liabilities with respect to policy holders.

However, some types of asset management activities are similar to those provided by banks and other nonbank financial companies, and increasingly cut across the financial system in a variety of ways. For example, asset managers may create funds that can be close substitutes for the money-like liabilities created by banks; they engage in various forms of liquidity transformation, primarily, but not exclusively, through collective investment vehicles; and they provide liquidity to clients and to financial markets.

The diversity of these activities and the vulnerabilities they may create, either separately or in combination, has attracted attention to the potential implications of these activities for financial stability. Some activities highlighted in this report that could create vulnerabilities—if improperly managed or accompanied by the use of leverage, liquidity transformation, or funding mismatches—include risk-taking in separate accounts and reinvestment of cash collateral from securities lending.

Unfortunately, there are limitations to the data currently available to measure, analyze, and monitor asset management firms and their diverse activities, and to evaluate their implications for financial stability. These data gaps are not broadly recognized. Indeed, there is a spectrum of data availability among asset management activities. Mutual funds and other investment companies registered under the Investment Company Act of 1940 (1940 Act) publicly report data on their holdings; banks report aggregated data on collective investment funds in regulatory Call Reports; and regulators have recently begun to collect data regarding private funds and parallel accounts on Form PF, under a mandate included in the Dodd-Frank Act. However, data for separate accounts managed by U.S. asset managers are not reported publicly and their activities are less transparent than are those of registered funds. Such accounts, according to estimates below, include roughly two-fifths or more of total assets under management (AUM) in U.S. firms. Privately owned asset management firms, which include several of the largest in the U.S., do not disclose information comparable to the public financial reports filed by asset managers that are public companies or subsidiaries of public companies. Data on some activities—such as involvement in repo transactions and the reinvestment of cash collateral from securities lending—are incomplete, thereby limiting visibility into market practices.

Reflecting these issues, this report describes:

- the activities of asset management firms and the funds they manage;
- the key factors that make the industry vulnerable to shocks: (1) "reaching for yield" and herding behaviors; (2) redemption risk in collective investment vehicles; (3) leverage, which can amplify asset price movements and increase the potential for fire sales; and (4) firms as sources of risk;
- the key channels through which shocks can be transmitted: exposures across funds and firms and the impacts of fire sales; and
- the data available to measure those activities, vulnerabilities, and channels, and the nature of the gaps in those data.

The report does not focus on particular risks posed by money market funds. In November 2012, the Council released a detailed analysis of these funds and their risks, and the Securities and Exchange Commission (SEC) recently proposed additional reforms.[2] In addition, the activities and risks posed by hedge funds, private equity, and other private funds are not addressed in detail. Additional analysis will be conducted in conjunction with further analysis of data that these funds have begun to file on Form PF. The OFR, SEC, and Commodity Futures Trading Commission (CFTC) are currently evaluating these data for monitoring purposes.

INDUSTRY ACTIVITIES

Asset managers provide investment management services and ancillary services to clients as fiduciary agents. The diversity of clients' needs results in a wide variety of firm structures and business models, ranging from investment boutiques that focus on a single product or clientele to large, complex financial institutions that offer multiple services.

Many asset managers focus their investment strategies on a single asset class, such as equities or fixed income; examples include long-only equity mutual funds and municipal bond funds. Some focus on a style of investing within an asset class, such as large-capitalization growth or dividend-yielding U.S. equities. Other managers cover broad market areas, offering multiple strategies within a fund or family of funds, and provide custom "solution" investment services for clients.

The industry is highly competitive and, in some ways, highly concentrated. Economies of scale in portfolio management and administration, combined with index-based strategies, have increased industry concentration in recent years. The largest asset managers generally offer the most comprehensive, low-cost client solutions. At the end of 2012, the top five mutual fund complexes managed 49 percent ($6.6 trillion) of U.S. mutual fund assets, including 48 percent ($2.8 trillion) of equity funds and 53 percent ($1.7 trillion) of fixed income funds. The top 25 mutual fund complexes managed 74 percent ($9.9 trillion) of U.S. mutual fund assets, including 74 percent ($4.3 trillion) of equity funds and 75 percent ($2.5 trillion) of fixed-income funds.[3] Ten firms each have more than $1 trillion in global assets under management (AUM), including nine U.S.-based managers, as concentration in the sector has increased (see Figure 2). Higher concentrations could increase the market impact of firm-level risks, such as operational risk and investment risk, or increase the risk of fire sales.

This narrative makes clear that asset management firms have a diverse mix of businesses and business models, offer a broad variety of funds, and engage in many activities. This diversity suggests that asset management activities should be the analytical building blocks for understanding the industry. Such an approach permits the flexibility to analyze risks posed by firms (firm divisions, or firms as consolidated entities) or by industry market sectors by aggregating activities and assessing the interplay among them. Analyzing activities individually or in combination permits analysis of transmission channels for risks, as well as assessments of how industry or firm practices could amplify risks to financial markets, institutions, or funds.

Figures 1 through 3 provide an overview of the asset management industry and its firms and activities. Figure 1 illustrates broad categories of sources of investable assets and translates them into various types of investment vehicles through the managers that provide them. It is important to note that there is inherent double-counting in the figure due to cross-investing among managers and to the use of several data sources. Figure 2 provides estimates for the top 20 asset managers by AUM. The table illustrates that firms vary significantly in the extent of their unregistered investment management activities. Figure 3 illustrates for these firms their relationship with their parent companies. The figures underscore that most of the data available to analyze the industry relate to firms or funds, not to activities. This report proposes a framework for reconciling activities with firms and identifies the gaps in data that must be filled for that crosswalk.

Activities can be divided into functions performed at the client or fund level and those performed at the firm level. Activities at the fund level include asset allocation and security selection, as well as the management of fund liquidity and leverage. Portfolio managers allocate assets and select portfolio holdings according to the guidelines prescribed by a fund's prospectus or a separate account's investment management agreement. Figure 4 outlines business lines by significant asset class for large domestic asset managers. Activities undertaken at the firm level include centralized trading (including securities trading, derivatives trading, securities lending, and repo transactions), risk management, market and securities research, and administrative functions. Interconnections between fund- and firm-level activities are extensive; most funds rely on their sponsors for core services, and fund managers are typically employees of the advisory firm.

Risk management practices and structures vary significantly among firms. For example, although all registered investment companies and investment advisers are required by SEC regulation to have chief compliance officers, not all asset managers have chief risk officers.[4] Regardless of the structure used, effective risk management is important for the management of operational limits, counterparty limits, and investment concentrations across funds and accounts.

Some firms adopt a core investment strategy and implement that strategy across multiple funds and accounts. In addition, firms may offer strategies that seek to hedge risks across asset classes; for example, so-called risk-parity or all-weather funds combine equity and levered, fixed-income portfolios to achieve risk parity across the two asset classes.

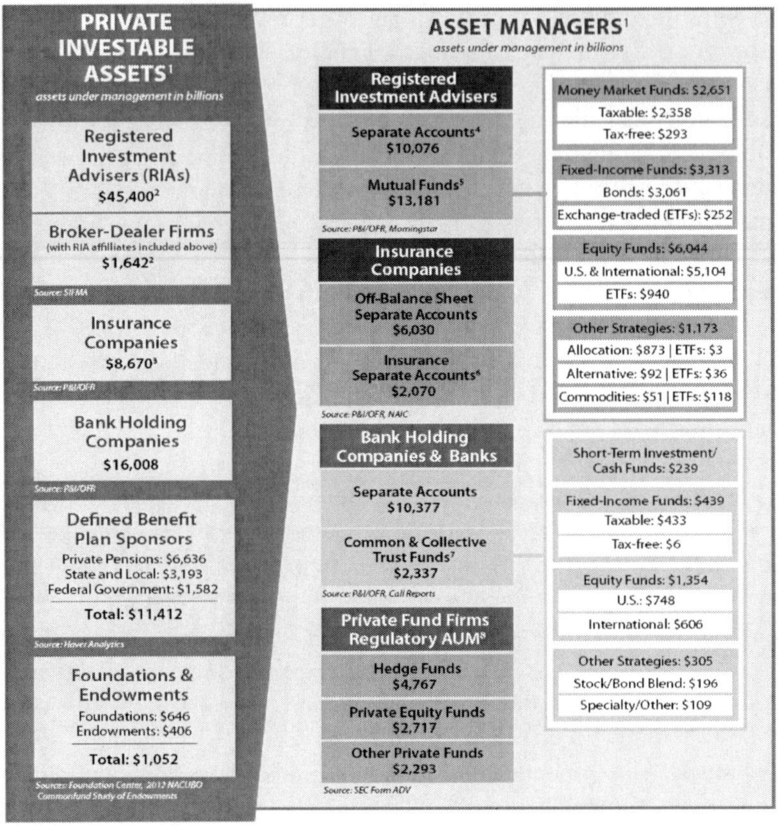

1 Figures include double-counting due to cross-investing among managers and multi-sourcing of data in construction of table.

2 Includes all non-exempt registered investment advisers as reported on the SEC's Form ADV.

3 Some insurance companies reporting data to Pensions & Investments (P&I) classify insurance separate accounts and other on-balance sheet assets as assets under management.

4 Separate accounts estimated by deducting registered funds from total world-wide assets under management using P&I data.

5 Mutual funds registered in the United States.

6 Separate accounts managed by an insurance company, in which the assets are on the insurance company's balance sheet.

7 Does not include state chartered limited purpose trust companies.

8 Regulatory AUM refers to gross assets under management, without adjusting for leverage.

Figure 1. Asset Management Industry Overview *(as of 12/31/2012).*

	Asset Managers	**Worldwide (WW) AUM** *$ in billions*	**WW Registered Funds AUM**[1] *$ in billions*	**Registered Funds AUM** *as % of WW AUM*	**WW Unregistered AUM**[2] *$ in billions*	**Unregistered AUM** *as % of WW AUM*
1	**BlackRock Inc.**	$3,791.6	$2,114.8	55.8%	$1,676.8	44.2%
2	**Vanguard Group Inc.**	$2,215.2	$2,124.3	95.9%	$90.9	4.1%
3	**State Street Global Advisors**	$2,086.2	$608.8	29.2%	$1,477.4	70.8%
4	**Fidelity Investments**	$1,888.3	$1,436.3	76.1%	$452.0	23.9%
5	**Pacific Investment Management Company LLC**	$1,624.3	$1,054.1	64.9%	$570.2	35.1%
6	**J.P. Morgan Asset Management**	$1,426.4	$742.1	52.0%	$684.3	48.0%
7	**BNY Mellon Asset Management**	$1,385.9	$490.7	35.4%	$895.2	64.6%
8	**Deutsche Asset & Wealth Management**	$1,244.4	$298.1[3]	24.0%	$946.4	76.0%
9	**Prudential Financial**	$1,060.3	$273.1	25.8%	$787.2	74.2%
10	**Capital Research & Management Company**	$1,045.6	$1,045.6	100.0%	$0.0	0.0%
11	**Amundi**	$959.8	$363.0	37.8%	$596.8	62.2%
12	**The Goldman Sachs Group Inc.**	$854.0	$338.0	39.6%	$516.0	60.4%
13	**Franklin Templeton Investments**	$781.8	$617.2	79.0%	$164.6	21.0%
14	**Northern Trust Global Investments**	$758.9	$152.9	20.1%	$606.0	79.9%
15	**Wellington Management Company LLP**	$757.7	$395.0	52.1%	$362.7	47.9%
16	**AXA Investment Managers**	$729.8	$203.3	27.9%	$526.6	72.1%
17	**Metlife Inc.**	$721.3	$0.0	0.0%	$721.3	100.0%
18	**Invesco**	$687.7	$443.8	64.5%	$243.9	35.5%
19	**Legg Mason Inc.**	$648.9	$353.6	54.5%	$295.3	45.5%
20	**UBS Global Asset Management**	$634.2	$12.1	1.9%	$622.2	98.1%

[1] WW Registered Funds AUM determined by summing P&I data on each asset manager's worldwide AUM and ETF AUM.

[2] WW Unregistered AUM determined by subtracting WW Registered Funds AUM from Worldwide AUM.

[3] For 2012, Deutsche Asset & Wealth Management declined to respond to the survey question on its registered funds, according to P&I. Its worldwide mutual fund AUM was $298.05 billion in 2011.

Sources: P&I, OFR Analysis

Figure 2. Top 20 Asset Managers by Assets Under Management *(as of 12/31/2012)*.

	Highest Level Asset Management Entity	Parent Company	Parent Entity Type
1	BlackRock Inc.	BlackRock Inc.	Domestic entity other
2	Vanguard Group Inc.	Vanguard Group Inc.	Non-deposit trust company- member
3	State Street Global Advisors	State Street Corp.	Domestic financial holding company
4	Fidelity Investments	Fidelity Management & Research LLC	Domestic entity other
5	Pacific Investment Management Company	Allianz Asset Management	Foreign insurance
6	J.P. Morgan Asset Management	JPMorgan Chase & Company	Domestic financial holding company
7	BNY Mellon Asset Management	Bank of New York Mellon Corp.	Domestic financial holding company
8	Deutsche Asset & Wealth Management	Deutsche Bank AG	Foreign financial holding company
9	Prudential Asset Management	Prudential Financial Inc.	Domestic entity other
10	Capital Research & Management Company	The Capital Group Cos. Inc.	Domestic entity other
11	Amundi	Credit Agricole S.A., Societe Generale	Foreign financial holding company
12	Goldman Sachs Asset Management	The Goldman Sachs Group Inc.	Domestic financial holding company
13	Franklin Templeton Investments	Franklin Resources Inc.	Domestic financial holding company
14	Northern Trust Global Investments	Northern Trust Corp.	Domestic financial holding company
15	Wellington Management	Wellington Management Company LLP	Registered investment adviser
16	AXA Investment Managers	AXA S.A.	Foreign insurance
17	Metlife Investment Management	MetLife Inc.	Domestic entity other
18	Invesco	Invesco Ltd.	Domestic entity other
19	Legg Mason Capital Management	Legg Mason Inc.	Registered investment adviser
20	UBS Global Asset Management	UBS AG	Foreign financial holding company

Note: Domestic entity other is a Federal Reserve System designation for any legal entity that is not a bank, bank branch, foreign bank, or bank holding company.

Sources: Federal Reserve, P&I, OFR Analysis.

Figure 3. Top 20 Asset Managers with Parent Company and Type.

Asset Managers	Alternatives	Equity	Fixed Income	Money Market Mutual Funds	Exchange Traded Funds	Collective Investment Trusts	Separate Accounts
BlackRock Inc.	x	x	x	x	x	x	x
BNY Mellon Asset Management	x	x	x	x		x	x
Capital Research & Management Company	o	x	x				o
Fidelity Investments		x	x	x		x	x
Franklin Templeton Investments		x	x				x
Goldman Sachs Asset Management	x	x	x	x			x
Invesco	x	x	x	x	x	x	x
J.P. Morgan Asset Management	x	x	x	x		x	x
Legg Mason Capital Management		x	x	x			x
Metlife Inc.	x		x			o	x
Northern Trust Global Investments	o	x	x	x		x	x
PIMCO	x		x				x
Prudential Asset Management		x	x				x
State Street Global Advisors		x	x	x	x	x	x
The Vanguard Group	o	x	x	x	x		o
Wellington Management	o	x	x				x

Note: This table is based on U.S.-domiciled markets; all asset managers listed except for Wellington Management manage money market funds; according to Morningstar, PIMCO had $9.1 billion under management in ETFs at the end of 2012.

x - signifies that AUM for a particular category was either greater than or equal to $50 billion.

o - signifies incomplete information.

Sources: Morningstar, SEC10-K and 10-Q filings, Bloomberg, Asset Managers' Websites, OFR Analysis

Figure 4. Significant Asset Class Business Lines of Large Domestic Asset Managers *(as of 12/31/2012)*.

Such strategies may also be offered through multiple channels. Other activities undertaken at the firm level may either help to manage risk or result in increased risk across the firm's activities, such as taking on leverage through unsecured borrowing, establishing and maintaining redemption lines of credit,[5] and managing proprietary investments.[6]

As described in the sections that follow, a certain combination of fund- and firm-level activities within a large, complex firm, or engagement by a significant number of asset managers in riskier activities, could pose, amplify, or transmit a threat to the financial system. These threats may be particularly acute when a small number of firms dominate a particular activity or fund offering. Connections between asset management activities and other market activities could contribute to the transmission or amplification of risks from one market sector to another, irrespective of whether those risks originated from asset managers. Activities aimed at boosting returns through leverage, such as the use of derivatives, reliance on borrowing, or other means discussed below, could contribute to system-wide leverage and risk transfer. Figure 5 illustrates the connections from activities to vulnerabilities and transmission channels.

VULNERABILITIES

Factors that make the industry vulnerable to financial shocks include (1) "reaching for yield" and herding behaviors; (2) redemption risk in collective investment vehicles; (3) leverage, which can amplify asset price movements and increase the potential for fire sales; and (4) firms as sources of risk.

Reaching for Yield and Herding

An extended low interest rate investment climate, low market volatility, or competitive factors may lead some portfolio managers to "reach for yield," that is, seek higher returns by purchasing relatively riskier assets than they would otherwise for a particular investment strategy.[7] Some asset managers may also crowd or "herd" into popular asset classes or securities regardless of the size or liquidity of those asset classes or securities.[8] These behaviors could contribute to increases in asset prices, as well as magnify market volatility and distress if the markets, or particular market segments, face a sudden shock.

The asset management industry has many practices and regulatory restrictions that can mitigate such risks. For example, fund- and firm-level investment risk management is intended to ensure that investments conform to investment mandates and that credit quality, asset concentrations, volatility, leverage, and other issues are appropriately managed. Independent risk managers can reduce the risk of overextending portfolio mandates when they are empowered to challenge investment decisions.

Registered funds are required to disclose information to investors about their risks, portfolio holdings, concentrations, and investment strategies. Registered investment advisers are required to disclose to their clients in their annual brochures their significant investment strategies and related risks. In addition, regulatory restrictions are designed to align the interests of investment advisers and their clients and mitigate conflicts of interest. Managers have strong incentives to provide clients investment strategies matching their risk-return profiles. Given that most asset managers earn fees based on the amount of assets under management and that clients may freely move their accounts to another adviser or fund, advisers have strong incentives to meet client expectations.

However, potential information disparities between investment advisers and their clients could undermine those mitigants in the industry. Specifically, investors might not fully recognize or appreciate the nature of risks taken by their portfolio managers, despite required disclosures and investment mandate restrictions.[9] In some cases, managers' incentives (for example, some performance fees) may be structured so that managers share investors'gains on the upside but do not share investors' losses on the downside, a situation that creates incentives to invest in riskier assets.[10]

Competitive pressures may also increase incentives for managers to take on extra risks. For example, research on mutual funds has shown that managers who are lagging their peers toward year-end often take more risks than managers who are outperforming.[11] Depending on the flexibility of investment mandates, managers may take risks that investors do not fully appreciate. If these risks suddenly become apparent, they could spur redemptions and a flight to quality, which could in turn trigger adverse market contagion as managers sell assets to meet those redemptions.[12]

Regulation of asset managers often focuses on limiting conflicts of interest between asset managers and their clients, which can help mitigate these risks. However, such regulation focuses on helping ensure that managers adhere to their clients' desired risk-return profiles, but does not always address collective action problems and other broader behavioral issues that can contribute to asset price bubbles or other market cycles.

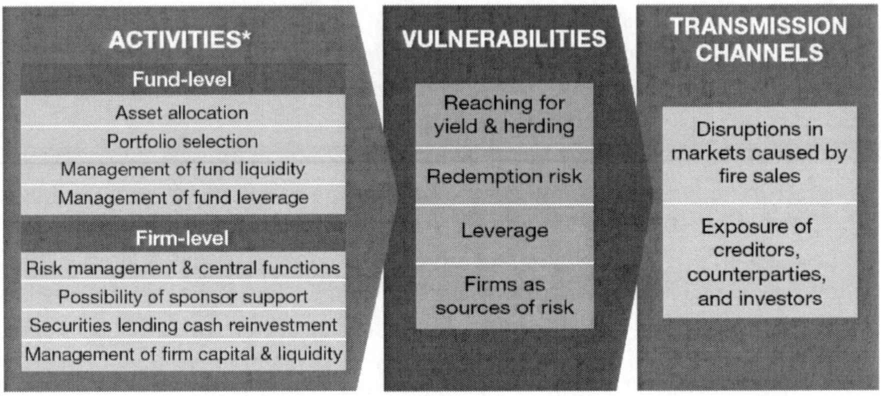

Example 1: Losses in highly leveraged funds, combined with reaching for yield behavior, could amplify fire sales and adversely affect fund counterparties.

Example 2: During a crisis, the rapid unwinding of investments of cash collateral from securities lending could pose risks that could amplify fire sales and trigger runs.*

* *The activities and examples are illustrative and not exhaustive.*

Figure 5. Asset Management Activities, Vulnerabilities, and Transmission Channels.

Competitive pressures can also be manifest in "herding"—the tendency of asset managers to crowd into similar, or even the same, assets at the same time. Such herding investment behavior in liquid assets may be unlikely to amplify financial stability shocks. Yet, herding into more illiquid investments may have a greater potential to create adverse market impacts if financial shocks trigger a reversal of the herding behavior. This behavior may occur because those assets appear to offer the best returns relative to the risks, but in other cases may result from competitive incentives or product types.

These potential risks could materialize in several different asset management activities. Pooled investment vehicles can potentially create market volatility and more rapid price impacts due to herding behaviors regarding investments in less liquid assets or increased redemptions due to shifting investments as risk tolerances or perceptions change.

For example, exchange traded funds (ETFs) may transmit or amplify financial shocks originating elsewhere.[13] These products have provided investors generally low-cost access to diversified investment portfolios and have grown rapidly, with $1.34 trillion in combined U.S. assets at the end of

2012, up from $102 billion in 2002.[14] Although the majority of ETF assets are invested in the very liquid equity market, ETFs also are used to obtain low-cost, diversified exposure to less liquid market segments, such as fixed-income securities, emerging market assets, and municipal bonds.[15] Low interest rates in recent years have contributed to the rapid growth in fixed-income ETFs, with assets growing from $57 billion at the end of 2008 to $252 billion at the end of 2012, although this product line is still relatively small compared to bond funds, which had over $3.1 trillion in assets at the end of 2012.[16]

The effects on market liquidity of trading in ETFs are ambiguous. On one hand, trading in ETF shares could improve price discovery in relatively illiquid markets by providing a market price for a portfolio whose underlying holdings are thinly traded. On the other hand, ETFs, like many pooled vehicles, could also potentially accelerate or amplify price movements in markets during market turbulence, thus reducing market liquidity. In such circumstances, market makers may step away from making markets because they do not have good and reliable pricing information regarding those underlying portfolio holdings.[17]

Volatility and tight markets also can have unexpected impacts on ETFs. For example, during market stress on June 20, 2013, an ETF authorized participant temporarily ceased transmitting redemption orders to various ETFs because the authorized participant had reached an internal net capital ceiling imposed by its corporate banking parent. During that same day, another ETF opted to redeem shares only in-kind (rather than make available a cash redemption option) because the transaction costs to redeem in cash had exceeded the costs that the ETF set for that day. In order to address the role that ETFs may potentially have in transmitting market stress going forward, it will be critical to study how the ETFs' capital markets service providers and partners (authorized participants and market makers) cope with market stress and volatility.

Another way that these risks could surface is by investors herding into certain new products, particularly if the products are relatively illiquid and investors fail to fully appreciate their risks under different market conditions.[18] In recent years, asset managers have developed registered funds that allow retail investors to gain exposure to certain alternative investment strategies more typically pursued by hedge funds. For example, certain hedge fund and private equity fund managers have introduced mutual funds that are managed using alternative strategies. Such funds can introduce more complex trading strategies and embedded leverage than traditional retail mutual funds do. During a market shock, when the risks become more apparent, investors who failed to appreciate the risks of these investments could engage in heavy redemptions of these products, exacerbating the shock.

It is important to recognize that asset managers can also have a stabilizing effect on the market. For example, asset managers with the financial strength and liquidity to buy assets trading significantly below their intrinsic values potentially could help to stabilize declines in prices.

Redemption Risk

Any collective investment vehicle offering unrestricted redemption rights could face the risk of large redemption requests in a stressed market if investors believe that they will gain an economic advantage by being the first to redeem.[19] Investors in mutual funds with portfolios of securities with varying levels of liquidity may have a "first-mover advantage" to sell early, if they believe cash on hand and maturing assets are insufficient to cover redemption requests and that more liquid assets may need to be sold to meet redemptions.[20] In a stressed market environment, this scenario could leave slower-to-redeem investors holding shares of an increasingly less liquid portfolio whose net asset value (NAV) may fall at an accelerating rate as market liquidity premiums rise. Asset sales in response to redemptions could also spread stress from certain types of portfolio assets to other portfolio assets and market segments.[21] Heightened redemptions from an asset manager's funds could increase market risks if there is a perception that the asset management firm itself is at risk of failure.

Fund managers use well-established liquidity management tools to manage and mitigate redemption risk. As a precaution against high demand for redemptions, funds often hold cash buffers and maintain liquidity lines of credit. To meet redemption requests, under SEC guidelines, registered mutual funds should hold at least 85 percent of their investments in assets that the fund manager believes could be sold at or near carrying value within seven days.[22] Funds may increase the proportion of the portfolio invested in more liquid securities if they anticipate market turbulence or another shock that could lead to heavier redemptions. Many funds also track their investor redemption behaviors and plan heavier portfolio liquidity around times when fund investors are more likely to redeem, such as when tax payments are due or in anticipation of year-end tax loss selling. Some large asset managers trade directly with other buy-side firms through "dark pool" exchanges, primarily as a means of seeking best execution, but also to guard against potential situations in which traditional third-party liquidity providers—particularly broker-dealers—are unable or unwilling to provide sufficient trade liquidity.

Registered funds have little ability to impose restrictions to prevent heavy redemptions in times of stress. Registered funds generally may not suspend investor redemptions, and must satisfy redemption requests within seven days. Many mutual funds disclose that they may pay back investors "in kind"—in securities rather than in cash—if they are under severe stress, although practical challenges have rendered this tool rarely used by funds, even in times of severe stress. Mutual funds generally would not be able to impose redemption fees to counter sudden heavy redemptions under existing regulations. In contrast, private funds are often structured to permit temporary suspensions of redemptions or the imposition of redemption fees or gates that limit redemptions in times of stress.

During normal market conditions, the availability of liquidity in capital markets allows managers to trade securities in response to varying investor fund flows. Institutional investors tend to have more predictable funding needs based on fixed expenditures or liabilities, facilitating liquidity management for institutional funds; on the other hand, they tend to be quicker than retail investors to pull their funds in a market downturn and take larger investment stakes. Although some fund managers may focus on holding more liquid assets, such as large capitalization stocks with narrow bid-ask spreads traded on multiple exchanges, others may focus on holding assets that are much less liquid, for example, collateralized loan obligations, emerging market equities, or thinly-traded corporate fixed income securities. If the liquidity of those assets varies significantly, and that variation widens under stress, fund investors in less liquid funds may perceive first-mover advantages to liquidating assets ahead of other investors. During the financial crisis, sophisticated investors tended to react more quickly to deteriorating market conditions than did retail investors, redeeming shares from funds more quickly if they perceived liquidity shortfalls.[23]

Figure 6 illustrates characteristics that make collective investment vehicles more vulnerable to redemption risks. On the vertical axis, risks are heightened for funds focused on preserving investor principal stability—such as money market funds or short-term investment funds (STIFs)—that offer daily liquidity to their investors.[24] Runs on such short-term funds can be self-reinforcing, as investor redemptions further drive down prices, returns, and liquid assets in the fund—spurring more redemptions. If perceived to have broader market implications, runs on these funds or groups of funds could contribute to risks of widespread fire sales.

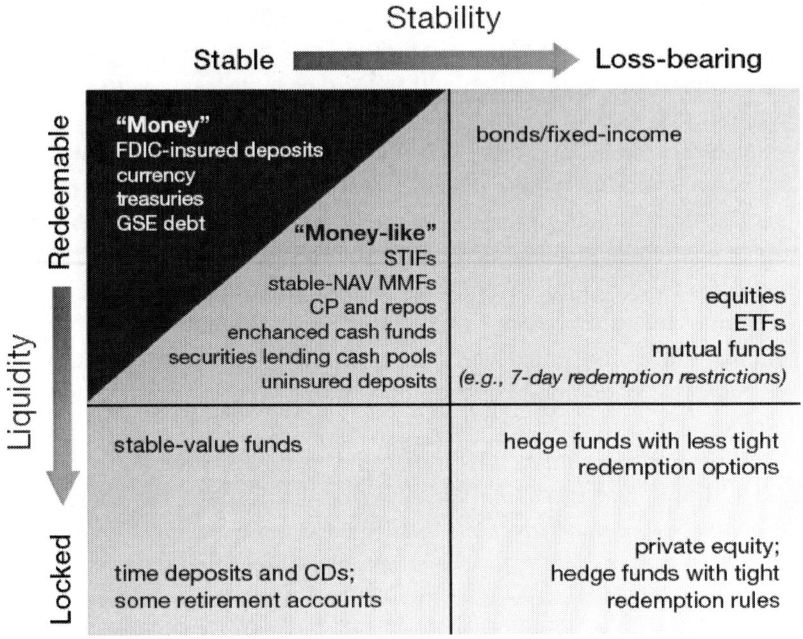

Source: OFR Analysis.

Figure 6. Investors' Liquidity and Stability Preferences.

Investors' concerns about the liquidity of one fund can quickly spread to similar or related funds, or to the sponsor of a fund complex. As an agency business, a financial services firm that suffers damage to its reputation through an extreme event in one business or fund may suffer redemptions or creditor pullbacks in its other funds or businesses. For example, investors in funds or accounts offered by a large asset management fund complex may react negatively together if the family is tainted by an operational failure, exposure of poor risk management practices, or collapse of a single fund. Although firm-specific problems are often attributed to firm idiosyncrasies and may not have broader market impacts, problems associated with an activity involving a large number of asset managers could affect market confidence and lead to redemptions.

The horizontal axis of Figure 6 categorizes funds by investors'stability preferences. In some circumstances, investors may believe that they can rely on sponsor support of the fund or product in a crisis, even in the absence of a legal or stated guarantee. They may hold this belief because of the way a product was marketed or because such support has been granted in the past.[25]

Although managers are not required to provide such support, competitive pressures or protecting firms' reputations may oblige it. Mutual funds and other types of products generally offer no guarantees that investors will be protected from principal loss, although many publicly-traded asset managers explicitly disclose in their regulatory filings (for example, Forms 10-K and 10-Q) that management reserves the right to provide support to any of their funds. In one example in November 2007, Bank of America supported investors in the $40 billion Strategic Cash Portfolio, then the largest enhanced cash fund in the country, and closed the fund after losses on mortgage-backed securities prompted the fund's largest investor to withdraw $20 billion.[26] In another example in November 2008, OppenheimerFunds contributed $150 million to a mutual fund to cover liquidity shortfalls due to derivatives exposures.[27] Direct and indirect support provided to investors in collective investment vehicles and separate accounts are not prominently disclosed, but, according to industry interviews, occurred during the crisis. Investors who expect their investments to be protected by explicit or implicit backstops could be expected to redeem funds in larger numbers if there is any sign that protections are eroding.

There are other possible scenarios in which redemption risk could amplify financial or economic shocks. If a number of funds were invested in similar assets or correlated assets, market events affecting that strategy or set of assets may affect and cause heavier redemptions in a number of funds, and sales of assets from any of those funds could create contagion effects on the related funds, spreading and amplifying the shock and its market impacts.

For example, a significant amount of assets has flowed into fixed income and hybrid mutual funds in the past five years (see Figure 7). As of 2012, 32 percent of mutual funds were bond and hybrid funds. Bond funds could be exposed to a risk of sudden price declines if interest rates were to suddenly rise.

In times of sharp changes in interest rates or related bond-market volatility, managers of these funds may be exposed to sudden heavier redemptions if they have not adequately managed the fund's liquidity, given market risks and the thinly traded nature of some fixed-income markets. Redemption risk is not prevalent in separate accounts because the assets are not managed in a collective investment vehicle. However, significant securities sales from separate accounts could still amplify a market impact.

Inadequate risk management relating to reinvestment of cash collateral for asset management securities lending programs illustrates how redemption-like risk can create contagion and amplify financial stability shocks.

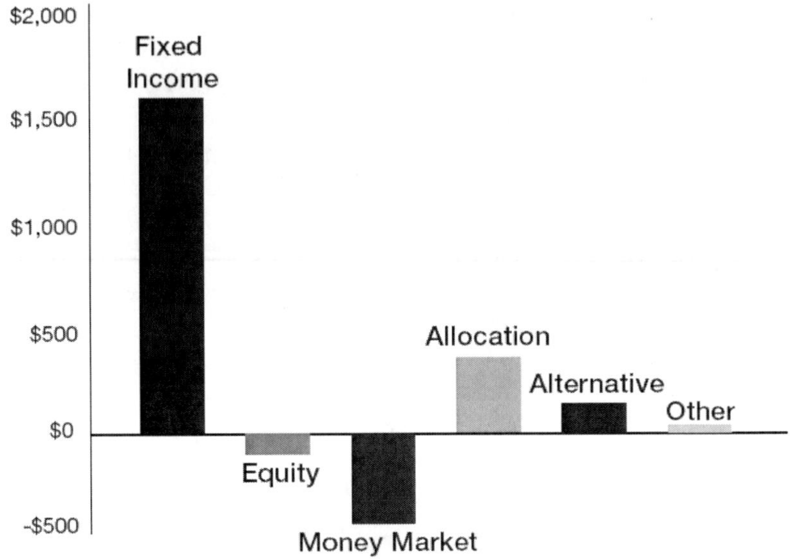

Source: Morningstar.

Figure 7. Net Worldwide Fund Flows, July 2008-June 2013 *(S in billions).*

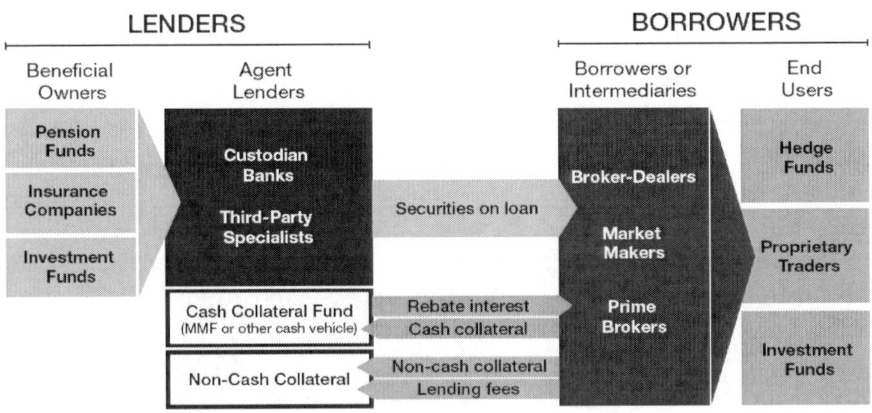

Sources: Bank of England (2011), OFR Analysis.

Figure 8. Securities Lending Transaction Flowchart.

Lending available securities on an over-collateralized basis was considered a low-risk method to earn incremental income for a fund or separate account before the financial crisis. In a securities lending transaction, a security is temporarily transferred to a securities borrower, who may use it for short-selling, hedging, dividend arbitrage, or market-making.[28] Securities lenders often share revenues with agent lenders, who broker transactions, provide accounting services, manage transactions, and often reinvest the cash collateral. Most agent lenders also provide indemnity for any borrower default by paying the lender for any collateral deficiency.

If securities lenders fear a loss of value in reinvested cash collateral due to market stress, they have an incentive to recall lent securities and exit reinvestment funds. Alternatively, borrowers may seek to return securities if they believe that their posted collateral may be at risk. The most prominent example during the crisis of inadequate risk management in cash collateral reinvestment occurred in the insurance context with AIG. Through a subsidiary, AIG Securities Lending Corporation, AIG ran a large securities lending business on behalf of its life insurance subsidiaries. AIG Securities Lending Corporation's cash collateral reinvestment practices, coupled with AIG's financial distress, caused it to sell assets that had become illiquid at a loss in order to return the cash collateral. This substantially contributed to AIG's losses.

This risk was not limited to AIG. Some asset managers also invested cash collateral in assets adversely affected by the financial crisis, such as structured investment vehicles and Lehman Brothers notes, and they provided financial support to those cash collateral reinvestment funds.[29]

The losses on cash collateral reinvestment amplified fire sales and runs during the crisis. They also contributed to the seizing of the money markets, in which cash collateral was typically invested. Daily marks and return of collateral due to the declining stock market further stressed the liquidity of collateral reinvestment funds.

Cash collateral reinvestment practices are not generally subject to comprehensive, targeted regulation and are not necessarily transparent to regulators or clients whose securities are lent. Due to data limitations, it is difficult to know, at any given time, the counterparty or risk exposures created by cash collateral reinvestment.

The connection between securities lending markets and cash collateral reinvestment, redemption risk, and short-term funding markets is not well understood and is difficult to measure due to a lack of comprehensive data.[30] When cash collateral is managed in separate accounts, visibility into these connections is reduced.

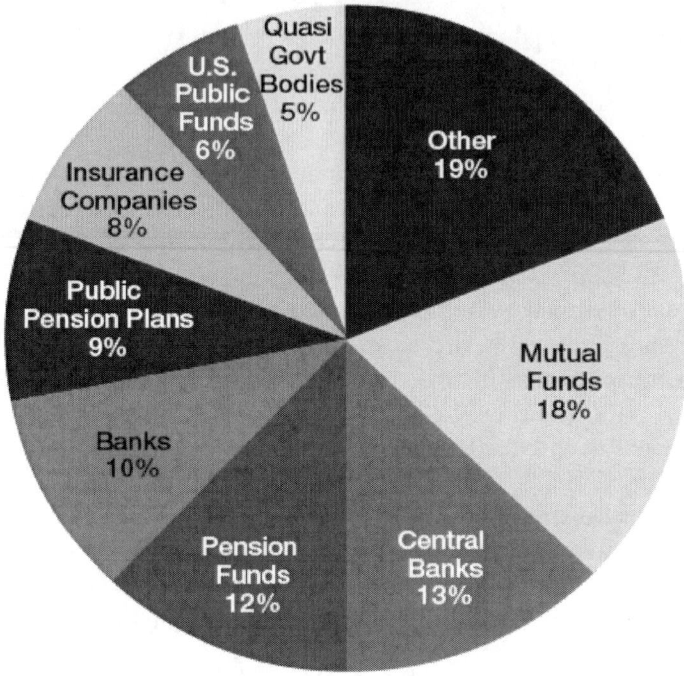

Source: Markit Group Limited.

Figure 9. Percent of Securities Lending Loans by Industry *(as of 3/25/2013).*

Leverage

The recent crisis illustrated that leverage, particularly short-term leverage, can subject borrowers to margin calls and liquidity constraints that increase the risk of fire sales.[31] In addition to borrowing, asset managers obtain leverage for their funds and accounts through derivatives (futures, options, and swaps), securities lending, and repurchase agreements.

Investors can obtain leverage through products such as leveraged or derivative-based ETFs or other exchange-traded products that can magnify gains and losses for the investor compared to the underlying index or portfolio assets. Asset managers can use leverage at the firm level (borrowing by the firm itself), the fund level (fund borrowing, or closed-end funds offering both common and preferred shares), or the portfolio level (acquiring leveraged, structured products or trading in derivatives).

Institutional investors and high-net-worth individuals face fewer limitations than smaller retail investors in obtaining leverage through managed funds and accounts. The Investment Company Act of 1940 (1940 Act) limits leverage levels for investment companies registered under that act. For example, mutual funds generally are required to hold assets equal to at least 300 percent of their bank debt, restricting leverage from bank debt to 33 percent of assets. Closed-end funds may also create leverage by issuing preferred shares.[32] However, unregistered funds and accounts are not subject to these regulatory restrictions.[33] Some complex trading strategies of such funds—such as "carry" trades in different currencies—often rely on leverage to boost returns.[34]

Registered funds also may incur additional leverage through the use of derivatives. Derivatives generally can create leverage by allowing funds to obtain exposure to market fluctuations in underlying reference assets—such as stock prices, commodity prices, or interest rates—that exceed the fund's investment in the derivative.[35] These transactions can either (1) result in the incurrence of potential debt obligations under the derivative contract, such as with a swap or future (indebtedness leverage), or (2) provide increased market exposure without the incurrence of future obligations, such as with a purchased option or structured note (economic leverage).[36] Registered funds are permitted to invest in derivatives, but are generally required to cover these positions with liquid assets equal to the indebtedness exposure created by the transaction; this cover requirement would either be the full obligation due at the end of the contract or, with respect to certain cash-settled derivatives, the daily mark-to-market liability, if any, of the fund under the derivative. Alternatively, a fund may be permitted to cover by holding an offsetting position that effectively eliminates the fund's exposure on the transaction. Cover is not required for instruments that create economic leverage but no indebtedness leverage.

Registered funds markedly expanded their exposure to credit derivatives in the run-up to the crisis. By 2008, 60 percent of the 100 largest U.S. corporate bond funds sold credit default swaps (CDS), up from 20 percent in 2004, according to a Federal Deposit Insurance Corporation working paper.[37] During the same period, the size of the average credit derivatives position in these funds grew from 2 percent to almost 14 percent, as measured by the notional value of the position relative to the fund's net asset value (NAV). The notional value exceeded 50 percent for six of the funds covered in the study. The study found that funds predominantly used CDS to increase their exposure to credit risks—that is, they were net sellers of credit protection, not net buyers.

During the financial crisis, the use of derivatives to boost leverage resulted in significant losses for some registered funds. For example, the Oppenheimer Champion Income Fund and Oppenheimer Core Bond Fund—two fixed-income retail mutual funds—lost roughly 80 percent and 36 percent of their NAV in 2008, respectively. The losses were primarily due to their exposure to total return swaps—a type of derivative in which investors exchange the total gains or losses from a reference asset without owning it—on AAA-rated tranched commercial mortgage-backed securities. OppenheimerFunds Inc., the funds' adviser, supported one of the funds that had insufficient liquidity to make payments related to margin calls on the risks associated with the swaps. The SEC later fined OppenheimerFunds $35 million for inadequately disclosing the risks associated with the leverage levels at the funds.[38]

In 2007, State Street paid significant settlements related to alleged fraudulent misrepresentations about the exposure of two funds to subprime mortgage credit risk and their use of leverage. The funds were leveraged approximately three-to-one through the use of total return swaps. These funds were unregistered collective investment funds managed by State Street Bank that targeted a stable NAV. Their leverage was unusually high for funds that were marketed as alternatives to money market funds, being more comparable to leverage employed at long/short hedge funds.[39]

The SEC issued a concept release in 2011 seeking public comment on the use of derivatives by registered funds. The release solicited comment on fund leverage, risk management practices, and derivatives exposure limits. Some of these potential options are similar to regulations recently implemented in Europe.[40]

As discussed below, data are currently insufficient to understand the exposures and the extent of leverage in separate accounts. As of earlier this year, Form PF requires all private funds to report data to the SEC related to their use of leverage.[41] The FSOC and the OFR have each noted the rationale and importance of monitoring leverage in the financial system in their annual reports to Congress.

Firms As Sources of Risk

The failure of a large asset management firm could be a source of risk, depending on its size, complexity, and the interaction among its various investment management strategies and activities. Distress at a large asset manager could amplify or transmit risks to other parts of the financial system. An asset manager's financial strength and reputation underpin its ability to attract clients, retain key employees, and deliver asset management services. Sponsors sometimes act in dual roles, as agents who provide portfolio management and other services, and as principals who may invest in their own funds or may provide implicit or explicit support to investors.

Concentration of risks among funds or activities within a firm may pose a threat to financial stability. Instability at a single asset manager could increase risks across the funds that it manages or across markets through its combination of activities.[42]

In a variety of ways, firms' risk managers could fail to understand or anticipate risks with financial stability implications. For example, a firm could manage a number of large, highly leveraged unregistered funds which have strategies that turn out to be correlated in ways firm risk managers did not anticipate, either because correlations shifted in times of stress or because the manager failed to consider certain factors that led to correlations among portfolio assets.[43] Similar concerns could arise if a firm with extensive repo and securities lending businesses, and that managed strategies with an array of interconnections through derivatives and other exposures, had difficulty unwinding or transferring clients' investments to another asset manager during a period of market weakness. Under stress, counter-parties also might not distinguish among exposures to the firm and its funds, and therefore could take risk-mitigating actions that could aggravate risks across the firm's funds and accounts.

Interconnectedness and complexity can transmit or amplify threats to financial stability; large financial companies tend to have multiple business lines that are interconnected in complex ways. The asset management division of a bank or insurance company may be linked to other financial market segments directly or indirectly through business connections within the firm. For example, some large, dedicated asset management companies offer comprehensive services through in-house broker-dealers, commodity pool operators, trust companies, or captive insurance divisions. Some offer broker-dealer, consulting, or pricing services to other asset managers, creating interconnections and dependencies that increase their importance in financial markets. Some large asset managers also have subsidiaries in many countries, complicating risk management and increasing the difficulty of supervision.

Asset Managers *$ in billions*	S&P Firm Rating	Assets under Management (AUM)	Money Market Fund (MMF) AUM	S&P Rating on Largest MMF	Book Value (BV)	Tangible Book Value (TBV)	AUM/BV	MMF AUM/BV
BlackRock	A+	3,792	264.0	AAA	25.40	(4.91)	149.27	10.38
Franklin Templeton Investments	AA-	782	5.7		9.20	7.06	84.97	0.62
Invesco	A-	688	73.0	AAA	8.32	(0.02)	82.69	8.81
Legg Mason Capital Management	BBB	643	124.0	AAA**	5.68	0.55	113.31	21.81
T. Rowe Price Group		577	15.0*		3.85	3.18	149.97	3.90
Affiliated Managers Group	BBB-	432	4.3*^		2.08	(1.86)	207.18	2.07
Federated Investors		380	285.0	AAA	0.50	(0.23)	766.61	574.66

Note: Data as of 4Q12, except if there is an asterisk.

* Data as of 3Q12.

** This is a Fitch rating.

^ Data estimated based on balance sheet (MMF AUM accounts for less than 1% of AUM).

Sources: S&P, SEC 10-K and 10-Q filings, Fitch, Moody's, OFR Analysis.

Figure 10. Book Value of Listed Asset Managers.

Moreover, material distress at the firm level, or firm failure, could increase the likelihood and magnitude of redemptions from a firm's managed assets, possibly aggravating market contagion or contributing to a broader loss of confidence in markets. The largest asset managers continue to win a significant share of the market, primarily by offering comprehensive solutions that benefit from established franchises and economies of scale.[44] Although separate accounts are typically easy to move from manager to manager due to separation of custody and management, if an investment adviser managed a large amount of separate account assets with complex, highly-customized strategies, a new manager may not be willing or able to quickly replace an existing manager during a period of market turbulence, or clients may require managers to liquidate assets prior to a transfer contributing to market risk.

Several large, complex financial institutions with asset management divisions suffered material distress during the recent crisis. Recent policy measures that seek to reduce these risks include heightened prudential standards for banks and designated nonbank financial companies and enhanced resolution authorities. During the crisis, stress spread between these companies'other businesses and their asset management subsidiaries. Heightened redemptions from the funds and accounts managed by the asset management divisions of Bear Stearns, Wachovia, and Lehman occurred in step with other destabilizing events in the market.

As agency businesses, asset management companies tend to have small balance sheets, and nonbank, non-insurance asset managers are not required by U.S. regulation to set aside liquidity or capital reserves for their asset management businesses.[45] The Federal Reserve's annual stress test requires the asset management divisions of large bank holding companies with money-like funds to set aside capital to cover the risk that they would have to support some of their funds during stress conditions. Figure 10 shows the book value of large dedicated asset managers compared to their assets under management—one indication of available firm resources. These resources can be used for operational purposes, as well as to seed new funds or potentially provide sponsor support to funds based on market circumstances.[46]

TRANSMISSION CHANNELS

Asset managers could transmit risks across the financial system through two primary channels: (1) Exposure of creditors, counterparties, investors, or other market participants to an asset manager or asset management activity, and (2) disruptions to financial markets caused by fire sales.

Exposure of Creditors, Counterparties, Investors, or Other Market Participants

The connections asset managers have with an array of financial companies, both within a holding company structure and with outside entities, could transmit risks among asset managers, other financial companies, and broader markets.

Direct connections among asset managers, banks, broker-dealers, insurance companies, and other financial services providers have grown over the past decade.[47] Banks and their subsidiaries are major service providers to the asset management industry, offering broker-dealer services, prime brokerage, fund accounting, custody services, and redemption lines of credit, as well as other forms of credit to funds and firms. Banks and insurance companies also serve as counterparties for various types of derivatives contracts and portfolio investments. Pricing providers offer valuation services enabling asset managers to mark their portfolios to market and calculate daily NAVs. Credit rating agencies also provide critical services. The extensive connections asset managers have with other financial services firms, and the concentration of some of these services, increase the potential that risks originating in other market sectors could be transmitted or amplified through asset managers into broader financial markets, or conversely, that risks originating in asset managers could be transmitted to other market sectors.

These industry linkages have increased the indirect connections among asset managers in recent years. Having common service providers, such as custodians, pricing providers, or securities lending brokers, or having common, large clients as investors, could result in common difficulties in the event of widespread service disruptions or redemptions. Fund-of-funds strategies that create implicit linkages between funds could also cause stress in the event of rapid redemptions, if severe price declines in more illiquid funds in the portfolio lead to increased selling pressure on more liquid funds.[48]

During interviews, asset managers suggested that counterparty risk management varies widely, with some firms establishing separate counterparty teams and others taking a fund-level approach subject to the discretion of portfolio managers. Funds are not specifically required to conduct ongoing credit analysis of their derivatives counterparties.

Disruptions to Financial Markets Caused by Fire Sales

Fire sales are rapid sales of assets that temporarily depress market prices, typically reflecting market participants' responses to market distress, including an escalating premium on liquidity and demand for it.[49] Higher demand for liquidity associated with fire sales can magnify and spread quickly across both asset classes and financial institutions, causing market prices to decline and market confidence to fall across market sectors.[50]

Fire sales can have a number of causes. Financial firms and market participants that use leverage or are required to maintain specific capital levels may be forced to sell assets at depressed prices if a decline in asset prices prompts higher haircuts or margin calls from creditors. Significant sales by a single large firm could depress asset valuation or increase market volatility, thereby transmitting stress to other institutions, which may then also face margin calls and be forced to sell assets, creating a knock-on effect. Alternatively, securities dealers having difficulty funding their activities may sell assets to generate liquidity, or investors in repurchase agreements may decide to sell collateral in the wake of a dealer default. Cascading effects from fire sales can amplify deterioration of market confidence and deepen a crisis.

In asset management, the following factors can increase the likelihood and severity of fire sales:

- **Large market positions and concentrations.** Fire sales may be exacerbated when a single fund or fund complex holds a large market position in a particular asset, sector, or strategy. This risk is heightened if the market has high informational or other barriers to entry; a lack of substitute investors could result in severe price depression if the fund or fund complex unwound its portfolio quickly. Asset managers managing large specialized funds and separate accounts with similar strategies may manage significant shares of important niche markets, which may not be fully transparent. Specialization concerns apply most directly to funds that focus on illiquid investments or funds that make large, concentrated bets.
- **Illiquid markets.** As markets become more illiquid, potentially due to market stress, they become increasingly prone to fire sales. Asset classes that tend to be less liquid include fixed-income securities, bank loans, and derivatives such as single-name credit default swaps. Customized or "bespoke" products can be particularly illiquid if they include complex combinations of derivatives and less liquid assets.

- **Reputation risk.** If an asset manager or one of its specialized funds suffers damage to its reputation, the redemption risk for the asset manager's funds could increase and heighten fire-sale risk. The potential asset pricing impact would be heightened if asset managers' funds and accounts held large positions in sectors with relatively low trading volumes, as in certain fixed income assets or markets.
- **Crowded trades.** Crowded trades can distort market prices and increase fire-sale risk. As discussed earlier, crowded trades occur when market participants have similar, correlated holdings in an asset class or trading strategy, and herding occurs. In the event of a shock, investors in crowded trades may try to sell or unwind their positions at the same time and in the same direction. Crowded trades may be especially problematic during a crisis, when few substitute investors may emerge to halt the downward spiral.
- **Leverage.** Excessive leverage can increase the risk that margin calls or other capital calls could prompt increased asset sales to cover positions. This risk is heightened in complex or less liquid funds, because price dislocation may be more severe, and during periods of market stress.
- **Transactions with liquidity "puts."** Certain transactions, such as securities lending and repo, have contractual obligations requiring liquidity upon demand and involve a large number of market participants. During periods of market stress, forced sales associated with these contractual obligations could increase the probability of fire sales.
- **Funding mismatches.** Short-term funding of long-term investments can lead to fire sales when funding liquidity is tight and investment values experience a negative shock.[51]

Mutual funds faced significant redemption requests during the crisis. According to Morningstar, redemptions from strategic income funds totaled $75 billion in the fourth quarter of 2008, nearly twice the volume during the quarter a year earlier, and redemptions by investors in government bond funds were $31 billion, 130 percent higher than during the fourth quarter of 2007. Although redemption risks that increase outflows from funds during periods of market stress do not necessarily pose threats themselves, they complicate liquidity management and can contribute to fire-sale risk.

According to some research, mutual funds in 2008 appeared to have been affected by fire-sale dynamics. Sharp declines in the value of their holdings of financial stocks may have compelled asset managers to sell off nonfinancial stocks in their portfolios as well. As evidence, researchers found in a 2012 paper that 10.5 percent of the 52 percent decline in the U.S. stock market related to the crisis could be attributed to distressed selling by mutual funds.[52] The paper noted, somewhat counter-intuitively, that this discount was highest for stocks that were considered stable and performed well before the crisis. In this way, funds sought to avoid realizing potentially large losses from selling stocks with the most depressed prices. Although this strategy had a stabilizing effect on the price of financial stocks, increased selling of nonfinancial stocks may have contributed to market weakness in other sectors.[53]

DATA GAPS

Significant data gaps impede effective macroprudential analysis and oversight of asset management firms and activities. Data gaps block regulators' and supervisors' view of risk-taking, leverage, and liquidity transformation across financial markets and hinder their ability to fully analyze the nature and extent of financial stability risks relating to the asset management industry.

This section highlights several areas in which better data collection could facilitate macroprudential analysis, oversight, and monitoring of asset management firms and activities. Although increased data reporting requirements impose costs on firms, the OFR and regulators with jurisdiction over the firms and their activities discussed below could consider the extent to which significant benefits to financial stability monitoring could merit such increased reporting.

Data Gaps in Separate Accounts

Registered investment advisers, banks, and insurance companies manage trillions of dollars in separate account assets; the top five asset management companies alone manage $5.5 trillion in separate accounts.[54] Data about the types of assets held in these accounts, their counterparty and other risk exposures, and amounts of leverage are limited. As a result, supervisors today are unable to fully assess the nature or extent of any financial stability risks that could be amplified or transmitted by the activities of these accounts.

In a separate account, an asset manager typically has discretion to select and manage assets on behalf of a large institutional investor or high net-worth individual under mandates defined in an investment management agreement (IMA). The client retains direct and sole ownership of the assets under management, which are typically held at an independent custodian on behalf of the client. Because separate accounts are not collective investment vehicles that pool together a variety of investors'assets (and thus, there is no shared risk or vulnerability to other shareholders' redemptions), separate accounts are not subject to restrictions under the 1940 Act, such as those relating to investment concentration or leverage. Rather, their ability to take on leverage or to invest in various asset classes or concentrated positions is specified in the IMA and thus is contractually agreed between the asset manager and the client.

In addition, advisers to separate accounts are regulated under the Investment Advisers Act of 1940, applicable bank fiduciary regulations, and applicable state investment adviser regulations (or other similar regulations). Private pension plans, which are often separate account clients, are required to abide by guidelines established by the Department of Labor under the Employee Retirement Income Security Act (ERISA). Although these regulators typically collect information about these advisers' assets under management, types of clients, and types of advisory activities, they do not routinely collect information about separate account holdings, leverage, risk exposures, or liquidity. In addition, although securities supervisors periodically examine asset managers that they regulate, including any separate accounts they manage, they normally focus their examinations on ensuring that the manager adheres to fiduciary obligations, investor protection regulations, and contractual agreements such as the IMA.[55]

As a result of this regulatory framework, data to analyze aggregate exposures and asset holdings of separate accounts across asset management complexes are limited. Some private data providers gather data on separate accounts, but asset managers provide these data only on a voluntary basis and these data are inconsistent.

For a number of reasons, collecting additional data on leverage practices and risk exposures in separate accounts could be useful for financial stability monitoring. First, in some cases separate accounts are largely "clones" of existing strategies of funds managed by the asset manager, with small adjustments. Therefore, if the manager makes a shift in strategy in response to a financial shock, these clone accounts can magnify the impact of this strategy shift beyond the impact from its managed funds. Thus, separate accounts can potentially magnify the impacts from herding behavior.

In other cases, separate accounts can contain highly bespoke strategies that diverge significantly from registered fund strategies. For example, to generate higher returns for investors that would like to take on more risk than a pooled investment vehicle, a separate account manager might create a highly customized strategy involving illiquid securities or additional leverage.[56] These strategies can be idiosyncratic, and thus tend to diversify risk in the financial system and mitigate financial stability risks. However, if a number of large separate accounts take similar positions, particularly if highly leveraged or in a concentrated relatively illiquid market, those accounts could potentially help magnify or transmit financial stability shocks.

Given the limitations of existing data, the potential ways that separate account exposures or asset sales could affect markets are not adequately understood. Filling gaps in these data would allow for better macroprudential monitoring of related risks.

Data Gaps in Securities Lending and Repo Markets

As noted earlier, monitoring the reinvestment of cash collateral from securities lending is important for financial stability purposes, but such monitoring is limited by a lack of data. Collecting transaction level and position data on securities lending between large international financial institutions, including the composition of the underlying cash collateral reinvestment assets, would improve regulators' visibility into market activities.[57] Section 984 of the Dodd-Frank Act requires the SEC to adopt rules increasing the transparency of information about securities lending available to broker-dealers and investors. Such a rulemaking could fi ll some of the data gaps described earlier.

Similar concerns exist regarding the involvement of asset managers in repo activity. During a period of market stress in which funding liquidity is drying up, firms with large repo books and an array of interconnections may have difficulty unwinding clients' investments quickly.[58] Because such a situation could dislocate markets and heighten fire-sale risk, data on repo activity are critical to monitoring developments that could indicate stress.[59] Currently, many repo transactions can be monitored only indirectly.[60] Although the SEC is considering approaches to enhance transparency in the closely related securities lending market, collecting data at the transaction level and position level on the overall volume of repo transactions in all three market segments—the tri-party, bilateral (that is, transactions settled between dealers on a delivery versus payment basis), and general collateral markets—would provide regulators a holistic view of asset managers, as well as interconnections and concentrations within repo markets.[61]

Data Gap	Data Currently Available	Data Required	Data Use
Private Companies	Some limited reviews by credit rating firms (some issue debt privately)	Financial statements of firms with standard notes	- Assess the financial standing of firms - Identify activities undertakenby firms
Separate Accounts	Self-reported aggregates with limited/inconsistent detail on strategies	Description of strategies and holdings	- Identify market concentrations by firm
Securities Lending	Market volumes and securities on loan	Data identifying beneficial owners lending activity	- Identify participants in market - Assess potential threat of material unwind in activity by fund and firm-lender concentrations
Repurchase Agreements	Volumes by firm settled at tri-party agents	Volume in bilateral settlement by fund/account	- Aggregate view of asset managers participation in market - Identify concentrations

Figure 11. Data Gaps.

Data Gaps at the Firm Level

Many of the largest asset managers are private and do not issue public financial statements. Assessing their financial positions and constructing a complete picture of their activities and interconnections is difficult, if not impossible. Lack of data on these firms limits the ability to assess their financial condition or identify activities, such as excessive borrowing or liquidity transformation, that could pose a threat to financial stability. Given that many large asset managers are private, cross-industry measurements of fundamental metrics, such as overall leverage, are difficult to calculate, which complicates effective macroprudential oversight.

APPENDIX: ASSET MANAGEMENT FIRMS AND ACTIVITIES

Firm Types

Figure 1 displays the major participants in the asset management industry. Three kinds of firms are prominent:

- **Banks.** Banks often have asset management divisions through which they offer depositors and other customers'fiduciary services such as investment funds, wealth management services, trust services, and retirement products. These services may be offered through separate accounts or funds such as bank common trust funds or collective investment funds. A bank's investment management activities are exempt from SEC registration requirements unless the bank provides those services to an SEC-registered investment company, such as a mutual fund. In general, bank asset management activities are off-balance sheet.
- **Insurance companies.** Insurance companies often have asset management divisions that provide investment management and other services, such as retirement plans and guaranteed payments to clients. A number of insurance companies have acquired asset managers in recent years to expand their asset management businesses. For example, Allianz acquired PIMCO and AXA acquired AllianceBernstein. Insurance companies'asset management activities are distinct from their on-balance sheet insurance activities, such as those in their general accounts or associated with certain insurance separate accounts.
- **Dedicated asset management companies.** Dedicated asset management companies have two characteristics: (1) their main business is asset management, and (2) they are not integrated divisions of a bank or insurance company.[62] Although dedicated asset management companies are not regulated as bank holding companies by the Federal Reserve, many of them maintain a trust bank, regulated by the Office of the Comptroller of the Currency or a state bank regulatory agency, to offer collective investment funds to eligible

clients or certain individual retirement account products, as required under ERISA. Several are very large organizations involved in disparate businesses, servicing many types of clients and offering services similar to those offered by banks. Some are publicly traded, while others are privately held and do not provide publicly available, consolidated financial statements. Most dedicated asset management companies are registered with, and regulated by, the SEC as investment advisers.

Fund Types

There are four primary fund types in the industry:

- **Registered investment companies** are registered under the Investment Company Act of 1940 (1940 Act). They are required to abide by strict rules governing safekeeping and proper valuation of assets, transactions with affiliates, governance for fund management, use of leverage, and availability of liquidity, among other requirements. Registered investment companies include mutual funds, ETFs, closed-end funds, and unit investment trusts.
- **Private funds,** such as hedge funds and private equity funds, are excluded from registration under the 1940 Act, but advisers to these funds are generally required to register with the SEC or a state securities regulator.
- **Bank common and collective investment funds** are similarly excluded from rules under the 1940 Act, but, as noted earlier, are often subject to rules established by banking regulators.
- **Separate accounts** are accounts in which an asset manager selects assets on behalf of large institutional investors or high net-worth individuals under mandates defined in an investment management agreement. Clients retain direct and sole ownership of assets under management. Separate accounts are not specifically regulated under the 1940 Act, the Securities Act of 1933, or bank-specific regulations, although managers of those accounts are often registered investment advisers required to register with the SEC or a state securities regulator.[63]

REFERENCES

Adam, Tim, and Andre Guettler. "The Use of Credit Default Swaps by U.S. Fixed-Income Mutual Funds." Working Paper No. 2011-01, Washington, D.C.: FDIC Center for Financial Research, November 19, 2010.

Adrian, Tobias, Brian Begalle, Adam Copeland, and Antoine Martin. "Repo and Securities Lending." Staff Report no. 529, New York: Federal Reserve Bank of New York, December 2011. Revised February 2013.

Bank of England. "Developments in the global securities lending market." Quarterly Bulletin 51, no. 3 (2011): 224-233.

Begalle, Brian J., Antoine Martin, James McAndrews, and Susan McLaughlin. "The Risk of Fire Sales in the Tri-Party Repo Market." Staff Report No. 616, New York: Federal Reserve Bank of New York, May 2013.

Bernanke, Ben S. "Monitoring the Financial System." Speech at the 49th Annual Conference on Bank Structure and Competition sponsored by the Federal Reserve Bank of Chicago, Chicago, May 10, 2013.

Bhattacharya, Utpal, Jung Hoon Lee, and Veronika Krepely Pool. "Conflicting Family Values in Mutual Fund Families." *Journal of Finance* 68, no. 1 (2013): 173-200.

Billio, Monica, Mila Getmansky, Andrew W. Lo, and Loriana Pelizzon. "Econometric Measures of Connectedness and Systemic Risk in the Finance and Insurance Sectors." MIT Sloan Research Paper No. 4774-10, Cambridge, Mass.: MIT, November 1, 2011.

Boyson, Nicole, Christoff Stahel, and Rene Stulz. "Hedge Fund Contagion and Liquidity Shocks." *Journal of Finance* 65, no. 5 (2010): 1789-1816.

Brady, Steffanie, Ken Anadu, and Nathaniel Cooper. "The Stability of Prime Money Market Mutual Funds: Sponsor Support from 2007 to 2011." Working Paper RPA 12-3, Boston: Federal Reserve Bank of Boston, August 13, 2012.

Brown, Keith C., W. V. Harlow, and Laura T. Starks. "Of Tournaments and Temptations: An Analysis of Managerial Incentives in the Mutual Fund Industry." *Journal of Finance* 51, no. 1 (1996): 85-110.

Brunnermeier, Markus K., and Lasse H. Pedersen. "Market Liquidity and Funding Liquidity." *Review of Financial Studies* 22, no. 6 (2009): 2201-2238.

Chen, Qi, Itay Goldstein, and Wei Jiang. "Payoff Complementarities and Financial Fragility: Evidence from Mutual Fund Outflows." *Journal of Financial Economics* 97, (2010): 239-262.

Chevalier, Judith, and Glenn Ellison. "Risk Taking by Mutual Funds as a Response to Incentives." *Journal of Political Economy* 105, no. 6 (1997): 1167-1200.

Committee of European Securities Regulators. *CESR's Guidelines on Risk Measurement and the Calculation of Global Exposure and Counterparty Risk for UCITS.* Paris: CESR, July 28, 2010.

Coval, Joshua, and Erik Stafford. "Asset fire sales (and purchases) in equity markets." *Journal of Financial Economics* 86, no. 2 (2007): 479-512.

Covitz, Daniel, Nellie Liang, and Gustavo Suarez. "The Evolution of a Financial Crisis: Collapse of the Asset-Backed Commercial Paper Market." *Journal of Finance* 68, no. 3 (2013): 815-848.

Dasgupta, Amil, Andrea Prat, and Michela Verardo. "Institutional Trade Persistence and Long-Term Equity Returns." *Journal of Finance* 66, no. 2 (2011): 635-653.

Financial Services Authority. *Implementation of the Alternative Investment Fund Managers Directive.* Consultation Paper, London: FSA, November 14, 2012.

Financial Stability Board. *Strengthening Oversight and Regulation of Shadow Banking.* Consultative Document, FSB, November 18, 2012.

Financial Stability Board. *Strengthening Oversight and Regulation of Shadow Banking: Policy Framework for Addressing Shadow Banking Risks in Securities Lending and Repos and Policy Framework for Strengthening Oversight and Regulation of Shadow Banking Entities.* Consultative Documents, FSB, August 29, 2013.

Financial Stability Oversight Council. *2012 Annual Report.* Washington, D.C.: FSOC, 2012b.

Financial Stability Oversight Council. *2013 Annual Report.* Washington, D.C.: FSOC, 2013.

Financial Stability Oversight Council. *Authority to Require Supervision and Regulation of Certain Nonbank Financial Companies.* Final Rule and Interpretive Guidance, Federal Register 77, no. 70, April 11. Washington, D.C.: FSOC, 2012a, 21637-21662.

Financial Stability Oversight Council. *Proposed Recommendations Regarding Money Market Mutual Fund Reform.* Washington, D.C.: FSOC, November 2012, 2012c.

Gaspar, Jose-Miquel, Massimo Massa, and Pedro Matos. "Favoritism in Mutual Fund Families? Evidence on Strategic Cross-Fund Subsidiation." *Journal of Finance* 61, no. 1 (2006): 73-104.

Gennaioli, Nicola, Andrei Shleifer, and Robert Vishny. "Neglected Risks, Financial Innovation, and Financial Fragility." *Journal of Financial Economics* 104, no. 3 (2012): 453.

Grynbaum, Michael M. "Mortgage Crisis Forces the Closing of a Fund." *The New York Times,* December 11, 2007.

Hau, Harald, and Sandy Lai. "The Role of Equity Funds in the Financial Crisis Propagation." Research Paper No. 11-35, Geneva: Swiss Finance Institute, June 2, 2012.

Huang, Jennifer, Clemens Sialm, and Hanjiang Zhang. "Risk Shifting and Mutual Fund Performance." *Review of Financial Studies* 24, no. 8 (2011): 2515-2616.

Investment Company Institute. *2013 Investment Company Fact Book.* Washington, D.C.: ICI, 2013a. Investment Company Institute. *Exchange-Traded Fund Data June 2013.* Washington, D.C.: ICI, 2013b.

Jotikasthira, Chotibhak, Christian Lundblad, and Tarun Ramadorai. "Asset Fire Sales and Purchases and the International Transmission of Funding Shocks." *Journal of Finance* 67, no. 6 (2012): 2015-2050.

Keane, Frank M. "Securities Loans Collateralized by Cash: Reinvestment Risk, Run Risk, and Incentive Issues." Federal Reserve Bank of New York, *Current Issues in Economics and Finance* 19, no. 3 (2013).

Manconi, Alberto, Massimo Massa, and Ayako Yasuda. "The Role of Institutional Investors in Propagating the Crisis of 2007–2008." *Journal of Financial Economics* 104, no. 3 (2012): 491-518.

Martin, Antoine, David Skeie, and Ernst-Ludwig von Thadden. "Repo Runs." Staff Report no. 444, New York: Federal Reserve Bank of New York, April 2010, Revised January 2012.

Mitchell, Mark, Lasse H. Pedersen, and Todd Pulvino. "Slow Moving Capital." *American Economic Review* 97, no. 2 (2007): 215-220.

Office of the Comptroller of the Currency. *Comptroller's Handbook: Investment Management Services*. Washington, D.C.: OCC, 2001.

Office of the Comptroller of the Currency. *Short-Term Investment Funds.* Final Rule, Federal Register 77, no. 70, October 9. Washington, D.C.: OCC, 2012, 61229-61238.

Raddatz, Claudio, and Sergio L. Schmukler. "On the International Transmission of Shocks: Micro-Evidence from Mutual Fund Portfolios." *Journal of International Economics* 88, no. 2 (2012): 357-374.

Schmidt, Lawrence D. W., Allan G. Timmermann, and Russ R. Wermers. "Runs on Money Market Mutual Funds." Working paper, January 2, 2013.

Securities and Exchange Commission and Commodity Futures Trading Commission. *Findings Regarding the Market Events of May 6, 2010.* Washington, D.C.: SEC-CFTC, 2010. http://www.sec.gov/news/studies /2010/marketeventsreport.pdf (accessed January 15, 2013).

Securities and Exchange Commission. "OppenheimerFunds to Pay $35 Million to Settle SEC Charges for Misleading Statements during Financial Crisis." Press Release 2012-110, June 6, 2012. Washington, D.C.: SEC, 2012.

Securities and Exchange Commission. *Money Market Fund Reform.* Proposed Rule, Release No. 33-9408, IA-3616. Washington, D.C.: SEC, 2013.

Securities and Exchange Commission. *Mutual Funds and Derivative Instruments.* Division of Investment Management, September 26, 1994. Washington, D.C.: SEC, 1994.

Securities and Exchange Commission. *Revisions of Guidelines to Form N-1A.* Investment Company Act Release No. 18612, Federal Register 57, No. 55, March 20, 1992. Washington, D.C.: SEC, 1992, 9828-9829.

Securities and Exchange Commission. *Use of Derivatives by Investment Companies under the Investment Company Act of 1940.* Concept Release, Federal Register 76, no. 173, September 7, 2011. Washington, D.C.: SEC, 2011, 55237-55255.

Sias, Richard W. "Institutional Herding." *The Review of Financial Studies* 17, no. 1 (2004): 165-206.

Spatt, Chester S. "Conflicts of Interest in Asset Management." Speech at the Hedge Fund Regulation and Compliance Conference, New York, May 12, 2005.

Tarullo, Daniel K. "Dodd-Frank Implementation." Testimony before the Committee on Banking, Housing, and Urban Affairs, U.S. Senate, Washington, D.C., July 11, 2013.

Tarullo, Daniel K. "Shadow Banking After the Financial Crisis." Speech at the Federal Bank of San Francisco Conference on Challenges in Global Finance: The Role of Asia, San Francisco, June 12, 2012.

The Boston Consulting Group. "Global Asset Management 2013: Capitalizing on the Recovery." Boston: BCG, 2013. https://www.bcgperspectives.com /content/articles/financial_institutions_ global_asset_management_2013_ capitalizing_recovery/ (accessed July 12, 2013).

Thomsen, Linda C. "Testimony Concerning the SEC's Recent Actions With Respect to Auction Rate Securities." Testimony before the Committee on Financial Services, U.S. House of Representatives, Washington, D.C., September 18, 2008.

Wermers, Russ. "Mutual Fund Herding and the Impact on Stock Prices." *Journal of Finance 54,* no. 2 (1999): 581-622.

End Notes

[1] FSOC (2012a), p. 21644.

[2] FSOC (2012c); SEC (2013).

[3] Morningstar Direct.

[4] Investment Advisers Act, Rule 206(4)-7. Banks typically use different titles for employees performing these functions.

[5] A redemption line of credit, provided by the firm that sponsors a fund or by a third party such as a bank, offers funds the ability to borrow to cover investor redemptions. As such, redemption lines offer fund managers the flexibility to keep less cash on hand, creating potential liquidity risks in the event of a market decline.

[6] Fund management firms often make proprietary investments, for example, in the form of seed capital to new funds, although these investments tend to be small relative to client assets under management.

[7] FSOC (2013), pp. 44-46, pp. 143-144; FSOC (2012b), pp. 139-141.

[8] Wermers (1999); Sias (2004); Dasgupta, Prat, and Verardo (2011).

[9] Spatt (2005).

[10] Keane (2013); Huang, Sialm, and Zhang (2011).

[11] Chevalier and Ellison (1997); Brown, Harlow, and Starks (1996).

[12] Gennaioli, Shleifer, and Vishny (2012).

[13] ETFs combine features of a mutual fund, which can be purchased or redeemed at the end of each trading day at its NAV per share, with the intraday trading feature of a closed-end fund, whose shares trade throughout the trading day at market prices. Only financial institutions designated as "authorized participants" are permitted to purchase and redeem shares directly from the ETF, and they can do so only in large blocks (for example, 50,000 ETF shares) commonly called "creation units." To purchase shares from an ETF, an authorized participant assembles and deposits a designated basket of securities and cash with the fund in exchange for ETF shares. Once the authorized participant receives the ETF shares, it is free to sell the ETF shares in the secondary market to individual investors, institutions, or market makers in the ETF. The redemption process is the reverse of the creation process. An authorized participant buys a large block of ETF shares on the open market and delivers those shares to the fund. In return, the authorized participant receives a pre-defined basket of individual securities, or the cash equivalent. This "hybrid" structure creates an arbitrage opportunity that generally keeps the ETF's market price relatively close to the ETF's underlying value. Unlike in the case of mutual fund shares, other investors can purchase and sell ETF shares only in market transactions and cannot purchase or sell creation units.

[14] Investment Company Institute (2013a).

[15] In June 2013, ETFs invested in equities held $1.17 trillion in assets while fixed income ETFs held $244 billion in assets. Investment Company Institute (2013b).

[16] Morningstar Direct.

[17] The Flash Crash on May 6, 2010 demonstrated the role ETFs can play in transmitting price dislocations in a distressed market. During that event, two-thirds of the 21,000 trades

cancelled were trades in exchange-traded products. A joint SEC-CFTC report noted that "many of the securities experiencing the most severe price dislocations on May 6 were equity-based ETFs." The report also noted the liquidity mismatch between ETFs and the underlying securities: "Sell pressure that overwhelms immediately-available near-inside liquidity is less likely to be 'caught' by resting orders farther from the mid-quote in an ETF versus an individual stock." SEC-CFTC (2010).

[18] Gennaioli, Shleifer, and Vishny (2012).

[19] Mitchell, Pedersen, and Pulvino (2007).

[20] Chen, Goldstein, and Jiang (2010).

[21] Manconi, Massa, and Yasuda (2012).

[22] SEC (1992).

[23] Schmidt, Timmermann, and Wermers (2013).

[24] STIFs are a type of bank collective investment trust and are excluded from SEC registration and regulation under the 1940 Act; they are subject to rules established by banking regulators. The Office of the Comptroller of the Currency (OCC) introduced new rules to reduce risks in STIFs in 2012 (OCC, 2012). The SEC introduced new rules to reduce risks in money market mutual funds in 2010.

[25] Brady, Anadu, and Cooper (2012).

[26] Grynbaum (2007). Enhanced cash funds are short-term funds that seek to offer higher yields than typically achievable by money market funds.

[27] SEC (2012).

[28] If the borrower of the security is a broker-dealer, it can only use the borrowed security for certain permitted purposes under Regulation T.

[29] For example, the Mount Vernon Securities Lending Prime Portfolio obtained an SEC staff no-action letter to enter into a capital support agreement with its affiliate due to its holdings of Lehman Brothers Holdings, Inc. notes and shares in the Reserve Primary Fund. SEC staff no-action letters relating to funds are available at http://www.sec.gov/divisions/investment.shtml.

[30] Keane (2013).

[31] Brunnermeier and Pedersen (2009).

[32] Closed-end funds can employ higher levels of leverage than mutual funds. Prior to the financial crisis, preferred shareholders in closed-end funds had a total of $64 billion in auction-rate preferred shares outstanding (Thomsen, 2008). These shares represented leverage for common shareholders. These shares were similar to auction-rate securities in that the interest rate was determined in periodic auctions. The freezing of the market for auction-rate securities in February 2008 affected auction-rate preferred shares issued by closed-end funds, increasing interest rates on the securities to default rates. Dividends on common shares fell significantly. Managers of closed-end funds used various means to support preferred shareholders without hurting common shareholders.

[33] Although not subject to regulation, leverage levels for unregistered funds and accounts may be restricted under investment mandates.

[34] A carry trade involves borrowing in a low-interest-rate market, typically a source of short-term wholesale funding, and investing the proceeds in (longer-term) higher-yielding assets, sometimes in a different currency from that of the sources of funding. For example, in recent years, investors borrowed in the U.S. dollar-denominated repo market to invest in foreign currency bonds.

[35] Funds registered under the 1940 Act are required to submit semiannual disclosures of derivatives holdings to the SEC in Form N-Q, but more information would be required to analyze funds' derivatives exposures from a financial stability perspective.

[36] SEC (1994), pp. 22-23.

[37] Adam and Guettler (2010). In addition to seeking leverage, funds may invest in CDS to obtain exposure to issues that may be unavailable in cash markets.

[38] SEC (2012).

[39] State Street was cited by the State of Massachusetts for noncompliance with state disclosure requirements.

[40] SEC (2011); CESR (2010).

[41] Certain private funds are required to report their secured and unsecured borrowings (for example, through loans or repos) as well as their use of derivatives. Analysis of these data will allow regulators to determine the overall use of leverage by private funds.

[42] Bhattacharya, Lee, and Pool (2013); Gaspar, Massa, and Matos (2006).

[43] Boyson, Stahel, and Stulz (2010). Correlations typically rise in periods of stress, reducing the benefits of diversification.

[44] The top 10 incumbent U.S. managers took 65 percent of all net new fund assets among managers with positive net flows in 2012 (BCG, 2013).

[45] Nonbank fund managers in the United Kingdom are subject to prudential regulation and minimum capital requirements at the firm level. Those capital requirements are designed to cover emergency liquidity needs and are thus not comparable to regulatory capital requirements for banks and insurance companies (FSA, 2012).

[46] Tangible book value excludes goodwill and other intangible assets in the calculation of assets. Negative tangible book value does not mean that a firm lacks cash or liquidity reserves.

[47] Billio, Getmansky, Lo, and Pelizzon (2011).

[48] Bhattacharya, Lee, and Pool (2013).

[49] Begalle, Martin, McAndrews, and McLaughlin (2013).

[50] Coval and Stafford (2007); Jotikasthira, Lundblad, and Ramadorai (2012); Raddatz and Schmukler (2012).

[51] Boyson, Stahel, and Stulz (2010); Covitz, Liang, and Suarez (2013).

[52] Hau and Lai (2012).

[53] Manconi, Massa, and Yasuda (2012).

[54] Insurer separate accounts, which include on-balance-sheet liabilities on the part of the offering insurance company, are not included in this analysis.

[55] National bank examinations of separate accounts focus on a bank's fiduciary duties to its customers, risks associated with the investment portfolios of these accounts, and the overall risks posed, in aggregate, by investment concentrations in these accounts and similarly run collective investment vehicles (OCC, 2001).

[56] In one of our industry interviews, an asset manager noted that it was able to use separate accounts to replicate a hedge fund strategy that the manager did not offer to its fund investors.

[57] Such an approach is consistent with the Financial Stability Board's Workstream 5 policy framework for addressing risks in repos and securities lending (FSB, 2012 and 2013).

[58] FSOC (2013), pp. 133-134.

[59] Begalle, Martin, McAndrews, and McLaughlin (2013); Martin, Skeie, and von Thadden (2012).

[60] Tarullo (2013).

[61] Adrian, Begalle, Copeland, and Martin (2013) provide a template for needed data in both repo and securities lending; see also Bernanke (2013) and Tarullo (2012).

[62] Some dedicated asset management companies are autonomous subsidiaries of large financial firms, such as PIMCO with respect to Allianz, and BlackRock with respect to PNC. The assets of these subsidiaries are generally not included on the parent firm's balance sheet and general management is delegated to the subsidiary.

[63] Off-balance sheet separate accounts offered by asset managers differ from on-balance sheet separate accounts offered by insurance companies in that they generally do not have contracted manager liabilities. Insurance companies with asset management divisions often offer both asset management separate accounts (off-balance sheet) as well as insurance separate accounts (on-balance sheet).

In: Asset Management ...
Editor: Leah T. McLain
ISBN: 978-1-63117-722-4

Chapter 2

FINANCIAL STABILITY OVERSIGHT COUNCIL: A FRAMEWORK TO MITIGATE SYSTEMIC RISK*

Edward V. Murphy

SUMMARY

The Financial Stability Oversight Council (FSOC) was created by the Dodd-Frank Wall Street Reform and Consumer Protection Act (DFA; P.L. 111-203) in 2010 as part of a comprehensive reform of banking and securities market regulators. The council is charged with monitoring systemic risk in the financial system and coordinating several federal financial regulators.

The 113th Congress may wish to monitor the performance, rulemaking, and policy recommendations of the council.

This report describes the mission, membership, and scope of the FSOC. It provides an analysis of several major policy issues related to the FSOC that may come before the 113th Congress.

The DFA establishes a regulatory framework of which the FSOC is a consultative council. The new regulatory regime incorporates several policy tools to address systemic risk. The FSOC facilitates

* This is an edited, reformatted and augmented version of a Congressional Research Service publication, CRS Report for Congress R42083, prepared for Members and Committees of Congress, from www.crs.gov, dated May 21, 2013.

communication among financial regulators, collects and evaluates financial data to monitor systemic risk, and designates which financial institutions and financial market utilities will be subject to prudential regulation by the Federal Reserve Board (the Fed). Upon a determination of a threat to financial stability, a covered non-bank financial institution in danger of failing may under certain conditions be resolved by the Federal Deposit Insurance Corporation (FDIC), rather than through the bankruptcy process. The FSOC may under certain circumstances set aside some financial regulations for consumers if the rules create systemic risk.

The Office of Financial Research (OFR), a permanent staff of financial experts, supports the members of the FSOC. The OFR processes, monitors, and analyzes financial data gathered from member agencies and collected from reporting firms. The OFR contributes to the annual report issued by the FSOC. In the 2013 annual report, the OFR noted a number of positive trends, including increased capital levels and liquidity among financial intermediaries.

However, the 2013 report includes several areas of continuing concern. For example, several sources of wholesale funding (such as money market mutual funds and repurchase agreements) remain vulnerable to the risk of runs or fire sales. The housing finance system still relies on government support, although financial trends for the government-sponsored enterprises (GSEs) have improved. A number of operational issues, such as information technology and resilience against cyber-attacks, are ongoing concerns. Interest rates create additional concerns, including the reliability of benchmarks such as LIBOR, and the exposure of financial intermediaries to significant losses should market interest rates rise (sometimes referred to as yield spikes). Longterm budget issues, so-called fiscal imbalances, remain a concern although revenues have recently been rising as general economic conditions improve in the United States. Finally, the 2013 annual report discusses several factors in other countries that could negatively affect financial stability in the United States if conditions overseas deteriorate, including the resolution of European financial turmoil and Japanese macroeconomic policies.

This report is intended to be used as a reference by congressional staff working on financial issues. The macroeconomic policy rationales for various financial crisis-related issues are summarized, and a glossary is provided to assist in understanding technical terms. This report is not intended to be read from cover to cover, but instead may be more useful as issues related to the FSOC arise.

INTRODUCTION: THE REGULATION OF BANK AND NON-BANK FINANCIAL INSTITUTIONS

In 2010, the Dodd Frank Wall Street Reform and Consumer Protection Act (P.L. 111-203, 124 Stat 1394), also known as the Dodd-Frank Act (DFA), established a new regulatory framework to address financial market instability. Included in that framework was the creation of the Financial Stability Oversight Council (FSOC), which is composed of the heads of the agencies that regulate financial institutions and markets. *Table 1* lists the member agencies. The FSOC has its own permanent staff in the newly created Office of Financial Research (OFR) that collects data on the financial system and provides information and technical expertise to the FSOC. OFR is housed within the Department of the Treasury, although it is funded separately.

The FSOC is expected to facilitate communication among existing financial regulators intending to identify sources of financial instability that cross agency regulatory jurisdiction, or that reside in gaps in the financial regulatory framework. Congressional staff may be interested in the organization, actions, and assessments of the FSOC, especially if a systemic financial event were to occur, a covered non-bank financial institution were to fail, and when the Secretary of the Treasury offers testimony to Congress (which is required at least once per year when the annual report is released).

Table 1. Membership of the Financial Stability Oversight Council

Voting Members (Heads of)	Non-Voting Members
Department of the Treasury	Office of Financial Research (OFR)
Federal Reserve Board (FRB or the Fed)	Federal Insurance Office
Office of the Comptroller of the Currency (OCC)	A state insurance commissioner
Consumer Financial Protection Bureau (CFPB)	A state bank supervisor
Securities and Exchange Commission (SEC)	A state securities commissioner
Federal Deposit Insurance Corporation (FDIC)	
Commodity Futures Trading Commission (CFTC)	
Federal Housing Finance Agency (FHFA)	
National Credit Union Administration (NCUA)	
Insurance expert (Appointed by the President)	

Source: P.L. 111-203 §111(b).

The FSOC was created to address some of the perceived regulatory weaknesses that may have contributed to the magnitude of the financial crisis of 2008. These perceived weaknesses included identification of risks to the financial system as a whole; lack of coordination among financial regulators; inadequate supervision of large, complex financial institutions; and instabilities that might result from the failure or bankruptcy of a non-bank financial institution. The FSOC provides a common forum for financial regulators to evaluate and address risks to the stability of the financial system, including systemic risks that might emanate from less regulated non-bank financial institutions. The FSOC has the ability to classify (or "designate" as used in the law and this report) certain non-banks as systemic, and therefore subject to prudential supervision by the Federal Reserve (the Fed). Systemic firms with more than $50 billion in assets must also provide and maintain resolution plans (so-called living wills), which must be jointly approved by the Fed and the Federal Deposit Insurance Corporation (FDIC).

The DFA establishes a regulatory framework of which the FSOC is a consultative council. The new regulatory regime has six basic policy tools with which to pursue its mission.

1) *Coordination.* The council facilitates communication among the heads of financial regulators.
2) *Data collection and evaluation.* The FSOC has a permanent staff with the ability to gather confidential financial information and the staff of the OFR are to be experts in the financial field.
3) *Prudential regulation of certain non-banks.* The FSOC establishes the criteria and designates which firms will be subject to additional prudential regulation by the Fed, including capital requirements, asset tests, and similar safety and soundness regulations.
4) *Safety and Soundness Regulation of certain Financial Market Utilities.* The FSOC establishes the criteria and designates which financial market utilities be subjected to safety and soundness regulation. An example of a financial market utility would be an organization that provides settlement and clearing services.
5) *Resolution of non-banks.* Upon a determination of a threat to financial stability, a covered non-bank in danger of failing may under certain conditions be resolved by the FDIC rather than through the bankruptcy process.
6) *Evaluation of rules for consumer financial protection.* The FSOC may set aside some financial regulations for consumers if the rules might cause systemic risk, under certain circumstances.

Banks and Non-Banks in Financial Turmoil

The distinction between depository banks and non-bank financial firms is important to understanding the FSOC because many of the new powers attempt to create a regulatory and resolution regime for non-banks that is similar to the way depository banks are handled.

The term *bank*, in this context, generally refers to financial institutions with bank, thrift, or credit union charters that offer loans and raise a large proportion of their funds through insured deposits. Insured depository banks have prudential regulators who monitor their assets and liabilities, including the ability to prevent concentrations in particular types of loans or reliance on particular funding sources. Prudential regulators of banks coordinate through the Federal Financial Institutions Examinations Council (FFIEC). Resolution of failing depository banks is done administratively by the FDIC (or NCUA for credit unions), not through the bankruptcy courts. Banks generally have access to liquidity facilities, such as the Federal Reserve discount window.[1]

The term *non-bank* refers to financial institutions that offer loans or other sources of capital, but do not have a bank charter and do not rely on deposits for their own funding. Prior to the financial crisis of 2008, investment banks, such as Bear Stearns and Lehman Brothers, were examples of large, complex, non-bank financial institutions, even though in some cases they may have had relatively small subsidiaries that accepted deposits (technically "thrifts"). The insurance company American International Group (AIG) is another example of a large non-bank financial institution that had a relatively small subsidiary that accepted deposits. Authority to regulate non-bank thrifts and their holding companies had resided in the Office of Thrift Supervision (OTS). Some non-banks accepted prudential regulation by the Securities and Exchange Commission (SEC).[2] Bankruptcy courts were to handle failures among most non-banks, and non-bank subsidiaries of banks. The government-sponsored enterprises (GSEs), Fannie Mae and Freddie Mac, are large, complex financial institutions that did not accept deposits, but had their own prudential regulatory regime under the Office of Federal Housing Enterprise Oversight (now the Federal Housing Finance Agency, or FHFA).

As then-Federal Reserve Governor Donald Kohn evaluated lessons from the financial crisis, "We [the Fed] traditionally have provided backup liquidity to sound depository institutions. But in the crisis, to support financial markets, we had to provide liquidity to non-bank financial institutions as well."[3] In common parlance, people have sometimes referred to "too-big-to-fail" firms (TBTF), but what is typically meant are complex and interconnected financial institutions that may not rely on deposits for a large share of their funding, and whose failure may spread and magnify losses throughout the financial system—rather than absolute firm size. Governor Kohn expressed frustration for the perceived inadequacy of existing tools to deal with TBTF nonbanks.[4]

Mortgage and Financial Market Turmoil and Response Overview

Dissatisfaction with existing regulation grew with the progression of the mortgage crisis that began in August 2007, especially following extraordinary government support related to the failure of several large non-banks. Some of this support was designed to prevent some creditors of failing non-banks from protracted uncertainty in the bankruptcy courts or other resolution process. Similarly, for some qualified financial contracts, support may have been designed so that some creditors would not suffer losses in the bankruptcy process.[5] For example, in March 2008, losses on mortgage-related securities caused the distress sale of investment bank Bear Stearns. The Fed provided financial support for the purchase of Bear Stearns by JPMorgan, avoiding the bankruptcy courts. In July 2008, the GSEs, Fannie Mae and Freddie Mac, had trouble raising additional capital. Policymakers tried unsuccessfully to enhance investor confidence by pledging financial support for the GSEs. Despite this pledge, in September 2008, Fannie Mae and Freddie Mac were placed in conservatorship with explicit financial support from Treasury. Lehman Brothers failed shortly thereafter, and declared bankruptcy when no firm was willing to purchase the investment bank without additional public support, which was not forthcoming. AIG, one of the world's largest insurers, would have failed the day after Lehman Brothers. However, the Fed subsequently intervened on behalf of AIG, in this case avoiding a bankruptcy process.

Following the declaration of bankruptcy by Lehman Brothers, financial panic spread to other non-bank institutions and markets, with runs on money market mutual funds and repurchase agreements (also known as "repos"). Treasury offered a temporary guarantee program for money market mutual funds. In fall of 2008, Congress provided Treasury with up to $700 billion to address troubled assets (such as mortgages) in the financial system. Despite these interventions to recapitalize and restore confidence in financial institutions, damage to the broader economy (as measured by unemployment and lost output) was severe.[6]

Congress passed the DFA to reform the financial regulatory system. For banks that accept deposits insured by the FDIC, technically "insured depositories," the general prudential regulatory approach and resolution regimes were relatively unchanged, although two regulators of depositories were combined. For large, complex non-banks, the DFA instructs the FSOC to identify which firms are systemically important, designates the Fed as the prudential regulator of these firms, and authorizes the FDIC to resolve covered non-banks outside the bankruptcy courts under certain circumstances. Under the DFA, policymakers have tried to construct resolution regimes for both banks and non-bank financial firms that will dispel investor expectations that some firms are too big to fail (i.e., that policymakers will be unwilling to let the firms fail because of potential collateral damage caused by resorting to the bankruptcy process). The following sections provide more detail on the mission, members, and recommendations of the FSOC during the 113th Congress.

This report will discuss the FSOC's mission and issues it is intended to address in Section I, and the members and their roles in Section II. Section III will analyze the perceived threats to financial stability as identified in law and by the FSOC in its 2013 annual report.

I. Financial Stability Oversight Council Mission

Section 112 of DFA lists three purposes of the FSOC: (1) *identify risks* to the financial system that may arise from large, complex financial institutions; (2) *promote market discipline* by reducing expectations of federal financial support for failing institutions; and (3) *respond to emerging threats* to the stability of the U.S. financial system. Items (1) and (2) are arguably directed at minimizing the chances that particular firms will be viewed as too big to fail, or too connected to fail, or otherwise pose risks to the financial system. Item (3) is arguably a more general catch-all for any factors that might destabilize the financial system.

In instructing the FSOC to promote financial stability, the DFA uses the terms *financial stability* and *systemic risk* in several places. For example, Section 112 directs member agencies of the FSOC to state in writing whether the agency believes that all reasonable steps are being taken "to ensure financial stability and to mitigate systemic risk that would negatively affect the economy." However, the DFA does not define the terms *financial stability* or *systemic risk.*

Financial Stability

Although the DFA does not define financial stability, the first FSOC annual report (2011) described some essential features of stable financial systems. "A stable financial system should not be the source of, nor amplify the impact of, shocks."[7] According to its annual report, the FSOC believes that there are three main risks that a financial system might transmit shocks: (1) failure of a financial institution or a market participant to honor a contractual obligation, (2) deterioration in market functioning, and (3) disruptions in financial infrastructure.[8] Applying the FSOC's interpretation of financial stability as used in Title I of the DFA, the mission of the FSOC is to help avoid financial activities, practices, and regulations that might spread or magnify shocks to the financial system.

Systemic Risk

There is no single, commonly accepted definition of the term systemic risk among financial professionals. The FSOC annual reports address the definition of systemic risk as follows: "Although there is no one way to define systemic risk, all definitions attempt to capture risks to the stability of the financial system as a whole, as opposed to the risk facing individual financial institutions or market participants."[9] Possible features of systemic risks include externalities and the fallacy of composition. With externalities, there are costs or benefits of actions by financial market participants that are not borne by those participants. With fallacies of composition, what is true for each individual firm in isolation may not be true when all firms follow similar strategies—just as while one person standing in a crowded stadium sees better, that strategy will fail if everyone stands at the same time.

Channels of Risk Proliferation

To better analyze whether the FSOC's approach addresses commonly understood channels of risk proliferation, one might examine central bankers' views of ways that failing firms can damage financial stability. Federal Reserve Governor Daniel Tarullo identified four such ways that in his view are most common.[10] They are as follows:

- Domino effects occur when the failure of one firm causes its creditors to fail, which causes the creditors' creditors to fail, and so on.
- Fire sales may become reinforcing when a product serves as the collateral to finance itself or in markets in which participants must post risk-based margin. Fire sales may become self-reinforcing if failure to pay causes lenders to seize the collateral (the good itself), sell it at distressed prices, and thereby cause further losses on other holders of the asset. These holders may then default on their loans or fail to post margin.
- Contagion can occur if the failure of one firm is a signal to investors that firms in the same industry or with similar assets are likely to be in financial trouble. Contagion can result in the restriction of liquidity to other firms as possible counterparties shy away.
- The failure of critical functions can cause systemic risk if a firm provides a unique financial service with no close substitutes. For example, if a clearinghouse has a monopoly on settlement services for a market, and the clearinghouse fails, then other market participants may not be able to process their own transactions.

Three of the sources of systemic risk identified by Tarullo, domino effects, fire sales, and critical functions, depend upon a firm's connections to other firms. These three forms of interconnectedness will typically be correlated with the size and scope of the firm, at least in relation to its market or service. If potential creditors to large firms judge that governments are likely to intervene to prevent an eventual bankruptcy, then this lower perceived risk of default may result in creditors being willing to offer the firms loans on easier terms than their less interconnected competitors. Big firms may thus gain funding advantages over smaller competitors, reinforcing the tendency of these firms to grow relative to their markets. Systemic risk regulators may attempt to construct and estimate a firm-specific index of systemic risk arising from these three sources of instability.

The remaining source of systemic risk identified by Tarullo, contagion, is relatively independent of firm size and complexity. Like the death of a canary in a coal mine,[11] the failure of even the smallest firm may signal that large firms, if they are exposed to similar risks, may be in danger. Contagion is thus based on the information that a firm's failure provides to investors, rather than a specific transactions or interconnections of the failed firm. Tarullo interprets the run on money market mutual funds that occurred in September 2008 as contagion that had little to do with the size, complexity, or transparency of Lehman Brothers. Rather, in Tarullo's view, the failure of Lehman Brothers was a signal to investors that money market mutual funds exposed to holders of mortgage-related assets could be in financial trouble. If correct, it would be difficult to construct or estimate a firm-specific index of systemic risk arising from this type of contagion.

The next section discusses the membership of the FSOC, and the special roles that some members have with respect to these six policy tools.

II. FSOC Membership and Roles

The FSOC has 10 voting members and 5 nonvoting members. (See *Table 1* above for a complete listing.) The council is chaired by the Secretary of the Treasury. Voting members include prudential bank regulators (e.g., the Office of the Comptroller and the Currency [OCC] and the FDIC), securities market regulators (e.g., the Commodity Futures Trading Commission [CFTC] and the SEC), and an independent insurance expert appointed by the President, with Senate confirmation. The nonvoting members include state level representatives from bank, securities, and insurance regulators, as well as the directors from the OFR and the Federal Insurance Office (FIO).

Several agencies have special roles in addressing the kinds of systemic risks that the FSOC was designed to monitor. The DFA grants specific authority under certain circumstances for the Secretary of the Treasury, the Fed, and the FDIC to act without further approval from the FSOC as a whole. However, with regard to actions taken for particular firms, these three agencies will often be relying on shared FSOC resources, such as the information provided by the OFR, or will coordinate actions with the firm's primary regulator, which will typically be another agency represented on the FSOC. The following describes the Treasury Secretary's role as chair of the FSOC, the Fed's role as prudential regulator of firms designated systemic by the FSOC, and the FDIC's role in resolving non-banks if the firm's failure is perceived as a threat to financial instability (not necessarily just firms designated as systemic). Whether the heads of these three agencies would be acting as members of FSOC, or in their agency's independent capacity, is beyond the scope of this report.

Secretary of the Treasury, Chair of the FSOC

The Secretary of the Treasury has a number of important functions on the FSOC that differ from the other members of the council. Foremost, the Secretary serves as the chair of the council. The chair has a number of powers and responsibilities related to FSOC meetings, congressional reports and testimony, and certain rulemakings and recommendations of the council. As chair, the Secretary may call a meeting of the FSOC.[12] Otherwise, meetings may be called by a majority of the members, but shall be held at least quarterly. The Secretary must testify before the House Committee on Financial Services and the Senate Committee on Banking, Housing, and Urban Affairs in conjunction with the release of the annual FSOC report. If any member agencies have notified Congress of deficiencies in systemic risk efforts, the Secretary is to address those concerns at the hearing.

The Secretary has special powers regarding the designation of systemic non-bank firms. Under Section 113(a)(1), a two-thirds vote of the FSOC is required to designate a non-bank as posing systemic risk and therefore subject to supervision by the Federal Reserve. However, one of the affirmative votes must be that of the Secretary of the Treasury. In other words, the chair of the FSOC has an effective veto over the designation of individual firms as systemically important; this applies to domestic and foreign firms, and for anti-evasion.[13] Similarly, the chair's vote is required to rescind or reevaluate the systemic designation of a firm. In emergencies, the chair's affirmative vote is required as part of the determination that a non-bank will not be granted the usual hearing before its designation as systemic. As part of those anti-evasion provisions, if certain large recipients of Troubled Asset Relief Program (TARP) funds (specifically, if they hold over $50 billion and were part of the Capital Purchase Program) cease to be bank holding companies, then they are automatically considered a systemically significant firm as if they had been designated as such by the FSOC and are placed under Fed supervision.[14]

As chair of the FSOC, the Secretary also has the responsibility to conduct or coordinate and report on periodic studies of the economic impact of systemic risk regulations.[15] These reports must be completed at least every five years. The Secretary of the Treasury has a consultative role with the OFR, which is responsible for certain research functions related to those reports and in other areas.

The Secretary, along with the Fed, negotiates with foreign regulators and multilateral organizations to coordinate prudential supervision and regulation for all highly leveraged and interconnected financial companies.

The Secretary plays a role in recommending receivership procedures for failing firms that have been designated as systemic. Although the Fed and the FDIC can make their own request for a receivership of a systemic firm based on evaluations described in Section 203a(2)(A-H), the Secretary may request a determination that a financial firm will default or is likely to default, with a systemic impact, and then appoint the FDIC as receiver. Note that the determination requires two-thirds vote of both the Fed and the FDIC board. In cases in which the firm is a broker-dealer, or its largest subsidiary is a broker-dealer, it is the Fed and the SEC by two-thirds vote that make the determination, in consultation with the FDIC. The Fed and the director of the Federal Insurance Office make the recommendation for insurance companies. The Secretary petitions the courts if the covered firm objects to the determination. The FDIC must consult with the Secretary to obtain a second extension of the time limit for the receivership.

Once a recommendation for receivership has been made, the Secretary is to make the determination and findings that trigger the resolution regime under the FDIC. The Secretary's determination must address (1) the likelihood that the firm will default or is in default; (2) the likely effect of the firm's failure on financial stability; (3) the viability of private sector alternatives available to prevent the default; (4) the impact on the firm's creditors and other counterparties; (5) the likelihood of FSOC resolution avoiding or mitigating systemic risks, its likely cost to the general fund of the Treasury, and the potential of receivership resulting in excessive risk taking by the firm or its creditors and other counterparties (i.e., moral hazard); (6) a federal regulatory agency has ordered the firm to convert all of its convertible debt instruments that are subject to the regulatory order; and (7) the company satisfies the definition of a financial company.[16]

The Secretary has a number of duties pertaining to the determination and procedures for the FDIC to act as receiver. First, the Secretary must notify certain majority and ranking members of Congress within 24 hours of the appointment of the FDIC as receiver. In addition, the rules and regulations that the FDIC issues for the use of funds pursuant to receivership must be acceptable to the Secretary.[17] The FDIC is to provide to the Secretary and the comptroller general an annual accounting report of receiverships. The Secretary's approval is required for the FDIC to provide additional payments[18] under some circumstances.[19]

The Secretary has a number of roles regarding orderly liquidation plans of covered institutions. Amounts from the resolution fund to support orderly liquidation under a liquidation plan must be acceptable to the Secretary.

Amendments to an orderly liquidation plan must be acceptable to the Secretary.[20] Furthermore, the FDIC is to assure the Secretary of a repayment plan for the orderly liquidation plan, and the Secretary and the FDIC must report to Congress on the terms of the repayment plan. To date, no firms have been subject to an orderly liquidation.

Federal Reserve—Prudential Regulator for Large Non-Banks

Since its creation in 1913, the Federal Reserve (the Fed) has had the authority to address financial market instability. Congress created the Fed as a lender of last resort following the recommendations of a commission established to investigate the causes of a financial panic that had occurred in 1907. Relative financial stability after WWII, and congressional directives to focus on price stability and maximum employment, may have redirected the Fed's focus to macroeconomic variables, but addressing financial market instability has always been a core mission of the Fed.[21] Under the FSOC, the Fed will not only be a lender of last resort, and conduct monetary policy, but the Fed will also have additional supervision and examination authority for individual non-banks designated by the FSOC.[22]

The Dodd-Frank Act directs the Fed to supervise certain large non-bank financial companies, but the FSOC recommends the standards. Section 115 of Dodd-Frank states that the regulatory standards for non-bank financial firms under Fed supervision must be more stringent than the standard for non-bank financial firms which are not under Fed supervision and do not present systemic risks. Section 115(b)(3) lists characteristics of non-bank firms that the Fed may supervise, including (1) risk-based capital requirements, (2) leverage limits, (3) liquidity requirements, (4) resolution plan and credit exposure report requirements; (5) concentration limits; (6) a contingent capital requirement, (7) enhanced public disclosures, (8) short-term debt limits, and (9) overall risk management requirements. Standards for foreign firms are to acknowledge equality of competitive opportunity and take into account the extent to which the foreign non-bank is subject to comparable standards in its home country.

The Fed has several powers and duties over covered bank holding companies and non-banks, upon a two-thirds vote of the FSOC.[23] For example, the Fed can limit the ability of the company to merge with other companies. It can restrict the products the firm offers, or impose conditions on the manner that the firm conducts activities. Under some circumstances, the Fed can require the company to sell or otherwise transfer assets or off-balance-sheet items to unaffiliated entities.

The Fed also has information collection authority, including through examinations, for covered firms, although the Fed is to rely on existing data sources to the extent possible.[24] In cases in which the covered firm has another primary regulator (such as the OCC), the Fed is to give the primary regulator reasonable notice of the proposed examination.

The DFA permits the Fed to establish standards for systemic firms in a number of additional areas.[25] These areas include a contingent capital requirement, enhanced public disclosures, short-term debt limits, and such other prudential standards as the Board of Governors, on its own or pursuant to a recommendation made by the FSOC, determines are appropriate.

FDIC Resolution Process for Certain Non-Banks

Since its inception, the FDIC has had the authority to administratively resolve insured depositories (banks and thrifts) that fail, rather than proceed through the bankruptcy courts. The DFA extends this authority to certain large and complex non-bank financial companies, under some circumstances.[26]

In addition to the Treasury Secretary's authority, the FDIC, with the concurrence of the Fed, may also recommend a determination of systemic risk from failing non-banks.[27] The FDIC's determination must include the votes of two-thirds of the FDIC's Board. Among the eight factors that the determination must address are

- the likelihood that the non-bank will default;
- a description of likely financial instability that could result from default;
- the recommended actions under liquidation authority; and
- an explanation of perceived deficiency of the bankruptcy process for this firm.[28]

Furthermore, Section 206 states that FDIC actions must be for the purpose of addressing systemic risk, and not be for the purpose of preserving the non-bank.

The powers and duties of the FDIC with respect to resolving systemic firms are set out in Section 210 of DFA. Essentially, the FDIC is the successor to the failing firm. The FDIC has the firms' rights, titles, and privileges. The

FDIC takes over its assets, with rights of collection. The FDIC takes over the functions of the firm's officers, directors, and shareholders. The FDIC has powers over any of the firms' subsidiaries that pose systemic risk. The FDIC can form bridge companies for the purpose of orderly liquidation. The FDIC is to pay valid obligations, subject to its systemic risk determinations. The FDIC's resolution is intended to ensure that shareholders and unsecured creditors bear losses. The FDIC may pay resolution costs as described in Section 204(d) of the DFA.

Once a resolution has been undertaken, the FDIC has reporting requirements to the FSOC and to Congress. After 60 days, the FDIC must deliver a written report to the appropriate congressional committees, providing additional details of the receivership. These additional details include but are not limited to (1) describing the financial condition of the failing firm at the time of receivership, (2) describing the FDIC's plan to resolve the failing firm, (3) describing the reasons for the provision of any funding to the receivership out of the Fund, and (4) explaining the expected costs of resolving the firm.

III. Analysis of Perceived Threats to Financial Stability

The FSOC's annual report to Congress is to include an analysis of perceived threats to the financial system. The following sections analyze specific threats mentioned in the 2013 FSOC annual report.[29] For each topic, the reader is provided a brief description of the issue, how it might contribute to a systemic event, and an analysis of the FSOC's report.

Vulnerabilities in Wholesale Funding Markets[30]

Issue Area

Although commercial banks raise significant funds through insured deposits, banks and other financial institutions also use a variety of other funding sources. Many of these alternative funding sources, often blending securities contracts and traditional loans, are categorized as *wholesale funding*. Examples of wholesale funding sources include money market mutual funds and repurchase agreements (repos). Wholesale funding sources are not eligible for certain government initiatives that assist financial stability, such as deposit insurance. Non-banks that use wholesale sources to fund capital market activity may be subject to runs similar to a depository bank, but would not typically have access to certain emergency lending facilities such as the Fed's discount window.

How It Might Go Wrong

Some wholesale funding markets can be subject to runs and fire sales. Banks and other financial intermediaries typically raise money in one market (such as deposits, repurchase agreements, and commercial paper) to fund activity in another (offer bank loans, capitalize securities investments, etc.). During periods of uncertainty and financial instability, financial intermediaries may lose trust in each other, and refuse to extend or roll over their loans to each other. The resulting reduction in wholesale funding can have many of the characteristics of a bank run by depositors if providers of wholesale funding fear that wholesale borrowers will not repay their obligations; but unlike deposits, sources of wholesale funding typically do not have any government guarantee.

A fire sale occurs when someone holding an asset must sell it in a distressed market even though a better price could likely be had if the seller had more time. Some wholesale sources of funding, such as repos and asset-backed commercial paper may be subject to fire sales. Collateralized lending can be subject to fire sales because borrower defaults are likely to occur at the same time that the market for the collateral is also distressed. As a result, when the lender seizes the collateral, the value of the collateral may be falling—the addition of the distress sales by lenders can magnify a downward spiral in prices. Both asset-backed commercial paper and repos use forms of collateral and may be subject to fire sales.

FSOC' s Perspective

The 2013 annual report notes some positive and negative developments (from the FSOC perspective) in wholesale funding. On the positive side, the annual report notes that intra-day credit exposure of the two clearing banks (JPMorgan and BNY Mellon) in the tri-party repo market has declined significantly. Similarly, the reliance of broker-dealers on overnight repos as a source of funding has also declined. However, the potential for runs on broker-dealers, or fire sales should there be a default by a major market participant, has not been completely eliminated. Furthermore, efforts to address potential instability in money market mutual funds have not as yet been finalized by the SEC (as regulator of MMFs as issuers of securities).

Housing Finance Reliance on Government Support[31]

Issue Area

Reliance on government assisted sources of funding increased markedly as a share of all mortgage funding in 2008. At the origination level, the mortgage market share of Federal Housing Administration (FHA) loans increased even for borrowers who could offer significant down payments with their house purchase. At the wholesale level, private mortgage securitization almost completely evaporated, making the government sponsored enterprises (GSEs) the dominant providers of wholesale mortgage funding. GSE funding has a variety of government support, including preferred stock purchases by the U.S. Treasury (through a conservatorship announced in September 2008), Federal Reserve purchases of corporate debt issued by the GSEs, and Federal Reserve purchases of mortgage-backed securities issued by the GSEs.

How It Might Go Wrong

The lack of significant private capital in mortgage funding is a sign that financial instability in mortgage markets has not yet completely healed (things already went wrong). It has been an announced goal of the FSOC to restore private capital as the primary source of long-term mortgage funding, along with improvements in consumer protection and financial stability. However, there are a number of signs that mortgage markets are improving. House prices have begun rising in a number of areas, default rates and foreclosures are no longer rising sharply, and the flow business (current mortgage revenues and guarantee fees compared with current payments) of the GSEs has been positive in recent quarters. One possible contributing factor for a delay in the return of private capital to mortgage markets (in addition to general pessimism about the speed of economic recovery in general and housing in particular) may be regulatory uncertainty as federal agencies implement changes to regulations related to the mortgage market.

FSOC' s Perspective

The 2013 annual report says that there has been significant improvement in mortgage markets, but additional progress is needed. On the positive side (from the FSOC's perspective), the conservatorship agreements (Treasury Preferred Stock Purchase Agreements, PSPAs) have been modified to expedite the wind-down of the retained portfolios of Fannie Mae and Freddie Mac. Regulatory uncertainty in mortgage markets may be reduced by the publication of final rules for the Real Estate Settlement Procedures Act

(RESPA), the Truth in Lending Act (TILA), and the Dodd-Frank Act's ability-to-pay standard. Additional work may need to be done to raise GSE guarantee fees to make room for private competitors to the GSEs.

Technology, Security, and Operational Risks[32]

Issue Area

The financial infrastructure can also be a source of systemic risk. This is essentially the "plumbing" of the financial system. It includes the environment in which financial trading occurs, communications of the interbank payment system, clearing and settlement of retail payments (including mobile payments), the security of confidential financial information, and the resilience of information storage systems. The "plumbing" of the financial system evolves with changes in communication technology and the organization of firms—historically, telegraphs, stock tickers, telephones, and computers have allowed for improved financial communications across long distances—but the stability of such systems can be threatened by the potential disruptions to the operational network.

How it Might Go Wrong

The financial infrastructure is vulnerable to natural disasters and human activity. For example, Hurricane Sandy temporarily halted trading on the New York Stock Exchange in October 2012. Malfunctions have disrupted the issuance of securities (such as the initial public offering of Facebook). Reportedly, major financial institutions have been subjected to attempts to access confidential information or disrupt their telecommunications (cyberattacks).

FSOC' s Perspective

The 2013 annual report noted several initiatives to address operational issues. For example as discussed in the wholesale funding section above, the tri-party repo task force has recommended improvements to the settlement and clearing processes in among the two central clearing banks to reduce their intra-day credit exposure. In the section of the 2013 report devoted to operational issues, the FSOC notes that the SEC recently proposed Regulation Systems Compliance and Integrity (Regulation SCI) to try to address malfunctions in capital markets.

Interest Rate Risks: Especially Rising Rates and Benchmarks[33]

Issue Area

Future interest rate changes may be a source of financial instability. A combination of a global savings glut, deficient aggregate demand, and central bank interest-rate policies have contributed to an extended period of low interest rates (by historical standards). At some point, interest rates are likely to rise, either because the demand for loanable funds rises as the economy improves driving up the rates or because a negative shock causes a spike in interest rates. Financial intermediaries, including but not limited to banks, can be damaged by rising interest rates if they have not adequately addressed the mismatch between the interest rates on their cost of funds and their revenues from longer-term lending. Furthermore, revelations of manipulation of the London Interbank Offer Rate (LIBOR) has cast doubt on the accuracy of key reference rates used to benchmark interest rates in many private contracts.

How It Might Go Wrong

There are several examples of rising interest rates contributing to stress in the financial system. Rising rates in the 1970s and 1980s created a great deal of stress for banks (especially savings and loans) that had funded long-term mortgages with short-term deposits. Rising rates in 1994 caused a significant sell-off in the bond market. Rising rates during 2004-2006 contributed to the end of the housing bubble (which would have ended eventually, but perhaps not at that time). Under-reporting of LIBOR rates in 2008 may have given financial regulators an overoptimistic view of the lending ability of major financial institutions during the liquidity crunch at that time.

There are several ways in which the current interest rate environment could contribute to financial instability. Low interest rates make it difficult for savers to earn significant returns with relative safety. For example, money market mutual funds are at greater risk because their income stream (from relatively safe bonds) is close to zero, which means that they are more likely to "break the buck" (return less than a dollar for each dollar invested) if any of their investments experience losses. Certain pension systems may find it difficult to earn adequate returns safely, especially if they have committed to defined benefits (a preset fixed payment) and have limited eligible investments. Other investors may have a greater temptation to "reach for yield" by investing in more risky categories of investments, increasing the likelihood of asset bubbles in other markets.

FSOC' s Perspective

In its 2013 report, the FSOC attributes current interest rates (low yields) to three factors. First, capital market participants forecast continued low interest rate policies by major central banks globally. The second is the pricing of short-term risk, which is partially caused by the increase in Treasury market purchases by institutions with low-risk sensitivity (including but not limited to central banks). The third factor cited by the FSOC is the willingness of bond market buyers to accept credit risk (i.e., the risk that borrowers will not pay back fully and on time). Provisions for credit losses and loan losses have declined recently.

The FSOC notes a number of initiatives to mitigate the risks when interest rates do rise. First, investigations and prosecutions related to LIBOR (and similar reference rates) may reduce the incentive to misreport, and combined with regulatory reform of reporting banks, may lead to more accurate interest rate benchmarks. The FSOC did express concern at potential reaches for yield, noting that the issuance of high yield bonds (riskier classes of bonds) had increased markedly, and that underwriting standards for collateralized loan obligations (CLOs) had reportedly loosened. Furthermore, threats to financial stability posed by rising rates are mitigated in part by one of the potential causes of rising rates—improved financial conditions. Even if rates rise for the "wrong" reason, a second credit crunch, the FSOC notes that the measurable financial resilience of major banks (such as capital levels and measures of liquidity) have improved.

Long-Term Fiscal Imbalances[34]

Issue Area

Fiscal policy refers to the relationship of government revenues and spending. Typically, recessions cause government revenues to decline and government spending to rise (fiscal policy expands). Economic booms can cause fiscal policy to contract if government revenues expand faster than government spending. Although recessions and booms cause fluctuations in short-term fiscal policy, long-term fiscal policy refers to the balance between expected government spending and revenues over an extended time horizon. CBO and other projections of long-term fiscal policy project an imbalance between expected federal revenues and expected federal spending for an extended period of time (spending commitments are greater than expected revenue streams). Thus far, the United States has not experienced any backlash in bond markets for running extended fiscal deficits. Not only has the yield on U.S. Treasury bonds remained low, but obligations of the United States have been viewed as a safe haven for some foreign investors and central banks.

How It Might Go Wrong

Fiscal imbalances can cause short-term problems and long-term problems. In the short run, governments with large fiscal imbalances run the risk that investors may suddenly demand higher yields to roll-over existing debt. Unlike Cyprus or Greece, short-term fiscal problems of the United States could be cushioned by purchases of Treasury securities by the Fed (which would be likely because a short-run fiscal crisis is often accompanied by the same kinds of poor economic conditions that cause the Fed to expand its monetary policies—although the early 1980s are a counter-example). In the longer term, the combination of higher interest rates and higher outstanding debt can cause interest payments to crowd out other government programs (depending on the relative growth of interest payments to GDP).

FSOC' s Perspective

The FSOC does not see a gradual normalization of long-term Treasury yields and volatilities as a significant threat to fiscal imbalances or the wider economy. However, the long-run imbalances could threaten financial instability if there is a sudden spike in yields. The FSOC notes that the financial impact of potentially disruptive short-run fiscal events has had "minimal impact"[35] thus far. For example, U.S. debt is still seen as a safe harbor despite the automatic tax increases and spending cuts at the start of 2013 (the fiscal cliff) and the February 2013 debt ceiling debates. Similarly, the downgrade of U.S. Treasury securities by Standard & Poor's did not cause a significant spike in Treasury yields.

Exposures to Risks from Other Countries[36]

Issue Area

Financial markets are global; therefore, financial instability overseas can threaten financial stability in the United States. There are many channels through which financial instability can cross borders. For example, the failure of a global bank could cause cross-border resolution issues, monetary policies of other countries can lead to competitive currency devaluations, capital flights away from some countries can cause global investment money (i.e., hot money) to flood other countries—and in some cases cause asset bubbles in the recipient country, and sovereign debt problems or banking policies in one country can cast doubt on the reliability of government debts or guarantees in other countries.

In introductory finance classes, sovereign debt of the governments of developed economies is often characterized as a risk-free asset. Recent events in Europe have cast serious doubt on this simplifying assumption. Changes in the perceived risk of the debt of sovereigns, such as Greece, Cyprus, Italy, Portugal, Ireland, are potential threats to financial stability in part because many financial regulators and financial institutions treat those debts as if they were risk-free. As a result, financial institutions and financial systems do not typically retain capital buffers against the possibility of sovereign debt restructuring, or in the extreme a sovereign default. The mere change in the perceived risk of sovereign debt can cause people to try to avoid institutions and markets with large exposure to that country's debt. At a minimum, exposed institutions may find it difficult to find counterparties for new transactions and may suffer withdrawals, or refusals to renew loans, from existing counterparties. The resulting financial instability can cause credit to dry up, interest rates to rise, and may magnify the financial difficulties of the sovereign experiencing the financial stress.

How It Might Go Wrong

Although financial regulators and Treasury officials in many countries have generally tried to coordinate their responses to the global financial crisis, there are a number of channels through which financial instability could be spread. First, there is no formal way to address a sovereign default (no international bankruptcy law applies to sovereigns), and thus European sovereign debt crises have been a series of evolving government funding and banking crises. Second, even if central banks target their domestic economies rather than their exchange rate, expansionary monetary policies can cause exchange rates to depreciate, and thus exports to rise and imports to fall. But one country's declining imports is another country's declining exports; therefore, expansionary monetary policies run the risk of competitive devaluation if policymakers fail to coordinate across countries.

FSOC' s Perspective

The 2013 FSOC report addressed several issues related to global financial stability. The FSOC noted a number of positive developments in Europe, including the potential for the European Central Bank (ECB) to purchase sovereign debt of member states under some circumstances. However, the report also noted that banking disruptions and policy responses in Cyprus (which briefly cast doubt on the status of insured bank deposits) create downside risk. The FSOC report also noted that austerity programs in Europe have "contributed to a contraction in euro-area economies," although euro area deficits may also have declined. The report also discussed expansionary monetary policies in Japan, which have contributed to a depreciation of the Yen. The FSOC took the view that "the U.S. has a strong financial stability interest in Japan finally escaping from deflation and securing more robust growth."[37]

APPENDIX A. GLOSSARY OF TERMS

This glossary has been compiled from several earlier CRS reports, the FCIC report, the CFTC and SIFMA websites, and from other sources.

Affiliate—A corporate relationship of control. Two companies are affiliated when one owns all or a large part of another, or when both are controlled by a third (holding) company (see "Subsidiary"). All subsidiaries are affiliates, but affiliates that are less than 50% controlled are usually not treated as subsidiaries.

Asset-backed security—A bond that represents a share in a pool of debt obligations or other assets. The holder is entitled to some part of the repayment flows from the underlying debt. (See "Securitization.")

Bank holding company—A business incorporated under state law, which controls through equity ownership ("holds") one or more banks and, often, other affiliates in financial services as allowed by its regulator, the Fed. On the federal level, these businesses are regulated through the Bank Holding Company Act.

Bank Holding Company Act—The federal statute under which the Fed regulates bank holding companies and financial holding companies (FHC). Besides the permissible financial activities enumerated in the Gramm-Leach-Bliley Act (P.L. 106-102), the law provides a mechanism between the Federal Reserve and the Department of the Treasury to decide what is an appropriate new financial activity for FHCs.

Blue sky laws—State statutes that govern the offering and selling of securities.

Broker/dealer—An individual or firm that buys and sells securities for itself as well as for customers. Broker/dealers are registered with the Securities and Exchange Commission.

Bubble—Self-reinforcing process in which the price of an asset exceeds its fundamental value for a sustained period, often followed by a rapid price decline. Speculative bubbles are usually associated with a "bandwagon" effect in which speculators rush to buy the commodity (in the case of futures, "to take positions") before the price trend ends, and an even greater rush to sell the commodity (unwind positions) when prices reverse.

Capital—Assets minus liabilities; what a firm owns minus what it owes. Regulators often require financial firms to hold minimum levels of capital.

Capital requirements—Capital is the owners' stake in an enterprise. It is a critical line of defense when losses occur, both in banking and nonbanking enterprises. Capital requirements help assure that losses that might occur will accrue to the institution incurring them. In the case of banking institutions experiencing problems, capital also serves as a buffer against losses to the federal deposit insurance funds.

Capital Purchase Program—Initiative under the Troubled Asset Relief Program providing financial assistance to U.S. financial institutions through the purchase of senior preferred shares in the corporations on standardized terms.

Charter conversion—Banking institutions may, with the approval of their regulators, switch their corporate form between: commercial bank or savings institution, National or State charter, and to stockholder ownership from depositor ownership. Various regulatory conditions may encourage switching.

Clearing Organization—An entity through which futures and other derivative transactions are cleared and settled. A clearing organization may be a division or affiliate of a particular exchange, or a freestanding entity. Also called a clearing house, multilateral clearing organization, or clearing association.

Collateralized debt obligation (CDO)—A bond created by the securitization of a pool of asset backed securities. (See CLO and CMO.)

Collateralized loan obligation (CLO)—A bond created by the securitization of a pool of loans, bonds, or asset backed securities. (See CDO and CMO.)

Collateralized mortgage obligation (CMO)—A multiclass bond backed by a pool of mortgage pass-through securities or mortgage loans.

Commercial bank—A deposit-taking institution that can make commercial loans, accept checking accounts, and whose deposits are insured by the Federal Deposit Insurance Corporation. National banks are chartered by the Office of the Comptroller of the Currency; state banks, by the individual states.

Commercial Paper Funding Facility Emergency Program—Created by the Fed in 2008, this program purchased three-month unsecured and asset-backed commercial paper from eligible companies.

Commodity Futures Modernization Act of 2000 (CFMA, P.L. 106-554, 114 Stat. 2763)— Overhauled the Commodity Exchange Act to create a flexible structure for the regulation of futures and options trading, and established a broad statutory exemption from regulation for OTC derivatives. Largely repealed by the Dodd-Frank Act.

Community Reinvestment Act 1977—A federal law which encouraged depository institutions to make loans and provide services in the local communities in which they take deposits.

Consolidated Supervised Entities program—A Securities and Exchange Commission program created in 2004 and terminated in 2008 that provided voluntary supervision for the five largest investment bank conglomerates.

Conservatorship—When an insolvent financial institution is reorganized by a regulator with the intent to restoring it to an ongoing business.

Counterparty—The opposite party in a bilateral agreement, contract, or transaction, such as a swap.

Credit Default Swap (CDS)—A tradeable contract in which one party agrees to pay another if a third party experiences a credit event, such as default on a debt obligation, bankruptcy, or credit rating downgrade.

Credit Rating Agency—Private company that evaluates the credit quality of securities and provides ratings on those securities; the largest are Fitch Ratings, Moody's Investors Service, and Standard & Poor's.

Credit Risk—The risk that a borrower will fail to repay a loan in full, or that a derivatives counterparty will default.

Credit union—A nonprofit financial cooperative of individuals with one or more common bonds (such as employment, labor union membership, or residence in the same neighborhood). May be state or nationally chartered. Credit unions accept deposits of members' savings and transaction balances in the form of share accounts, pay dividends (interest) on them out of earnings, and primarily provide consumer credit to members. The federal regulator for credit unions is the National Credit Union Administration.

Dealer—An individual or financial firm engaged in the purchase and sale of securities and commodities such as metals, foreign exchange, etc., for its own account and at its own risk as principal (see "Broker/dealer"). Commercial banks are typically limited to acting as dealers in specified high-quality debt obligations, such as those of the federal government.

Depository institution—Customarily refers to commercial banks, savings institutions, and credit unions, since traditionally the greater part of their funding has been in the form of deposits. Deposits are a customer's funds placed with an institution according to agreed on terms and conditions and represent a credit to the depositor.

Derivatives—Financial contracts whose value is linked to the price of an underlying commodity or financial variable (such as an interest rate, currency price, or stock index). Ownership of a derivative does not require the holder to actually buy or sell the underlying interest. Derivatives are used by hedgers, who seek to shift risk to others, and speculators, who can profit if they can successfully forecast price trends. Examples include futures contracts, options, and swaps.

Discount window—Figurative term for the Federal Reserve facility for extending credit directly to eligible depository institutions. It may be used to relieve temporary cash shortages at banks and other depository institutions. Borrowers are expected to have tried to borrow elsewhere first and must provide collateral as security for loans. The term derives from the practice whereby bankers would come to a Reserve Bank teller window to obtain credit in the early days of the Federal Reserve System.

Dual banking system—The phrase refers to the fact that banks may be either federally or state chartered. In the case of state-chartered banks, the state is the primary regulator; for national banks, the Office of the Comptroller of the Currency is the primary regulator.

Exchange—A central marketplace with established rules and regulations where buyers and sellers meet to trade futures and options contracts or securities.

Federal safety net—A broad term referring to protection of banking institutions through deposit insurance, discount window credit, other lender of last resort support, and certain forms of regulations to reduce risk. Commercial and industrial companies generally lack any of these cushions against loss.

Federal Open Market Committee—Its members are the Board of Governors of the Federal Reserve System and certain of the presidents of the Federal Reserve Banks; oversees market conditions and implements monetary policy through such means as setting interest rates.

Financial holding company—A holding company form authorized by the Gramm-Leach-Bliley Act (P.L. 106-102) that goes beyond the limits a of bank holding company. It can control one or more banks, securities firms, and insurance companies as permitted by law and/or regulation.

Financial institution—An enterprise that uses its funds chiefly to purchase financial assets such as loans and debt securities, as opposed to tangible property. Financial institutions are differentiated by the manner in which they invest their funds: in loans, bonds, stocks, or some combination; as well as by their sources of funds. Depository financial institutions are differentiated in that they may accept deposits which are federally insured against loss to the depositor. Non-depository financial institutions such as life and property/casualty insurance companies, pension funds, and mutual funds obtain funds through other types of receipts, whose values may fluctuate with market conditions.

Financial subsidiary—Under the Gramm-Leach-Bliley Act (P.L. 106-102), both national and state-chartered banks are authorized to form financial subsidiaries to engage in activities that would not otherwise be permitted within the bank itself, subject to certain limits. Besides the permissible financial activities enumerated in P.L. 106-102, the law provides a mechanism between the U.S. Department of the Treasury and the Federal Reserve to decide what is an appropriate new financial activity for a financial subsidiary.

Financial Stability Oversight Council—A council created by the Dodd-Frank Act (P.L. 111- 203) with identifying and monitoring systemic risks to the U.S. financial system, reducing expectations of extraordinary government intervention, and to respond to emerging threats to U.S. financial stability.

Firewalls—Barriers to the flow of capital, information, management, and other resources among business units owned by a common entity. In case of financial distress of one operation ("fire"), the "walls" are intended to prevent the spread of loss to the other units—especially to banking units. Example: losses in a securities subsidiary of a holding company could not be covered by any of the holding company's bank subsidiaries.

Foreign bank—Banks and their holding companies headquartered in other countries may have a variety of financial operations in the United States:

U.S.-chartered subsidiary banks, agencies, branches, and representative offices. Their primary federal regulator is the Federal Reserve, under the International Banking Act of 1978 as amended. States and the Office of the Comptroller of the Currency may also regulate them.

Functional regulation—Regulatory arrangements based on activity ("function") rather than organizational structure. The Gramm-Leach-Bliley Act (P.L. 106-102) called for more functional regulation than in the past.

Government-sponsored enterprise (GSE)—GSEs are private companies with government charters. Government sponsorship typically gives them a funding advantage over purely private competitors, while their charters restrict the kinds of businesses they may conduct.

Haircut—In computing the value of assets for purposes of capital, segregation, or margin requirements, a percentage reduction from the stated value (e.g., book value or market value) to account for possible declines in value that may occur before assets can be liquidated.

Hedge funds—Hedge funds are essentially unregulated mutual funds. They are pools of invested money that buy and sell stocks and bonds and many other assets, including precious metals, commodities, foreign currencies, and derivatives (contracts whose prices are derived from those of other financial instruments). Hedge funds are limited to qualified investors with high net worth.

Hedging—Investing with the intention of reducing the impact of adverse movements in interest rates, commodities, or securities prices. Typically, the hedging instrument gains value as the hedged item loses value, and vice versa.

Illiquid Assets—Assets that cannot be easily or quickly sold. **Insolvent**—A firm whose liabilities exceed its assets.

Institutional regulation—Regulation that is institution-specific as contrasted with activity specific (see "Functional regulation").

Investment bank—A financial intermediary, active in the securities business. Investment banking functions include underwriting (marketing newly registered securities to individual or institutional investors), counseling regarding merger and acquisition proposals, brokerage services, advice on corporate financing, and proprietary trading.

Investment bank holding company—A holding company for securities firms authorized under the Gramm-Leach-Bliley Act. Such holding companies are subject to regulation by the Securities and Exchange Commission.

Issuer—A person or entity (including a company or bank) that offers securities for sale. The issuing of securities, where the proceeds accrue to the issuer, is distinct from the secondary, or resale, market, where securities are traded among investors.

Lender of last resort—Governmental lender that acts as the ultimate source of credit in the financial system. In the United States, the Fed has this role.

Leverage—The ability to control large dollar amounts of a commodity or security with a comparatively small amount of capital. Leverage can be obtained through borrowing or the use of derivatives.

Liquidity—The ability to trade an asset quickly without significantly affecting its price, or the condition of a market with many buyers and sellers present. Also, the ability of a person or firm to access credit markets.

Liquidity risk—The possibility that the market for normally-liquid assets will suddenly dry up, leaving firms unable to convert assets into cash. Also, the risk that other firms will refuse to extend credit on any terms to a firm that is perceived as distressed.

Mark-to-Market—The process by which the reported amount of an asset is adjusted to reflect true the market value instead of the purchase price, or expected future sale price.

Market risk—The risk that the price of a tradeable security or asset will decline, resulting in a loss to the holder.

Money market mutual fund (MMF)—A form of mutual fund that pools funds of individuals and other investors for investment in high-grade, short-term debt and bank deposits paying market rates of return. Examples of these money market instruments include U.S. Treasury bills, certificates of deposit, and commercial paper. In addition to the investment features, most MMFs offer check-writing redemption features.

Moral hazard—The tendency of people to take more risks once another party has agreed to provide protection. Regulatory interventions to bail out failing firms are often said to create moral hazard, on the assumption that others will expect to be saved from their mistakes, too.

Mortgage-backed security (MBS)—A bond backed by a pool of mortgage loans. The bondholders receive a share of the interest and principal payments on the underlying mortgages. The cash flows may be divided among different classes of bonds, called tranches.

Mutual fund—An investing company that pools the funds of individuals and other investors, and uses them to purchase large amounts of debt or equity obligations of businesses and sometimes debt obligations of governments. The owners of the mutual fund hold proportional shares in the entire pool of securities in which a fund invests. Owners pay taxes on their distributions from a fund; the mutual fund itself is not normally subject to federal or state income taxation.

Naked option—The sale of a call or put option without holding an equal and opposite position in the underlying instrument.

Net Asset Value (or NAV)—Value of an asset minus any associated costs; for financial assets, typically changes each trading day.

Office of Financial Research (OFR)—An office created by the Dodd-Frank Act (P.L. 111-203) to support the Financial Stability Oversight Council and member agencies by collecting and standardizing financial data, performing applied and long-term research, developing tools for risk measurement and monitoring.

Operational risk—The possibility that a financial institution will suffer losses from a failure to process transactions properly, from accounting mistakes, from rogue traders or other forms of insider fraud, or from other causes arising inside the institution.

Over-the-counter (OTC)—Trading that does not occur on a centralized exchange or trading facility. OTC transactions can occur electronically or over the telephone.

Receivership—When an insolvent financial institution is taken over with the intent to liquidate its assets.

Repurchase Agreement (Repos)—A method of secured lending where the borrower sells securities to the lender as collateral and agrees to repurchase them at a higher price within a short period, often within one day.

Savings association—A savings and loan association, mutual savings bank, or federal savings bank, whose primary function has traditionally been to encourage personal saving (thrift) and home buying through mortgage lending. In recent years, such institutions' charters have been expanded to allow them to provide commercial loans and a broader range of consumer financial services. The federal regulator for most savings associations is the Office of Thrift Supervision. Also known as savings and loans, thrifts, and mutual savings banks.

Securities Investor Protection Corporation (SIPC)—A private nonprofit membership corporation set up under federal law to provide financial protection for the customers of failed brokers and/or dealers. SIPC is a liquidator; it has no supervisory or regulatory responsibilities for its members, nor is it authorized to bail out or in other ways assist a failing firm.

Securitization—The process of transforming a cash flow, typically from debt repayments, into a new marketable security. Holders of the securitized instrument receive interest and principal payments as the underlying loans are repaid. Types of loans that are frequently securitized are home mortgages, credit card receivables, student loans, small business loans, and car loans.

Shadow Banking—Financial institutions and activities that in some respects parallel banking activities but are subject to less regulation than commercial banks. Institutions include mutual funds, investment banks, and hedge funds.

Special-purpose entities (SPEs)—Also referred to as off–balance-sheet arrangements, SPEs are legal entities created to perform a specific financial function or transaction. They isolate financial risk from the sponsoring institution and provide less-expensive financing. The assets, liabilities, and cash flows of an SPE do not appear on the sponsoring institution's books.

Speculation—A venture or undertaking of an enterprising nature, especially one involving considerable financial risk on the chance of unusual profit.

State regulation—Under the dual system of bank regulation, states as well as the federal government may charter, regulate, and supervise depository institutions. States are the primary regulators in the insurance field. States also have authority over securities companies, mortgage lending companies, personal finance companies, and other types of companies offering financial services.

Structured debt—Debt that has been customized for the buyer, often by incorporating complex derivatives.

Subordinated debt—Debt over which senior debt takes priority. In the event of bankruptcy, subordinated debt holders receive payment only after senior debt claims are paid in full.

Subsidiary—A company whose controlling shares are owned 50% or more by another ("parent") corporation. Like companies with less than 50% ownership, it is an affiliate of the controlling company. A subsidiary is usually consolidated for regulatory and reporting purposes with its parent.

Systemic Risk—The term "systemic risk" does not have a single, agreed-upon definition. Some define systemic risk as the risk an institution faces that it cannot diversify against. In other circumstances, systemic risk is defined as the risk that the linkages between institutions may affect the financial system as a whole, through a dynamic sometimes referred to as contagion.

Thrift holding company—Also known as a savings and loan holding company, a business that controls one or more savings associations. These holding companies are regulated under the Home Owners' Loan Act by the Office of Thrift Supervision.

Too-big-to-fail doctrine—An implicit regulatory policy holding that very large financial institutions must be rescued by the government, because their failure would destabilize the entire financial system. (See "Moral hazard.")

Tri-Party Repo Market—A repurchase agreement in which a third party agrees to clear and settle the transaction and to monitor and assure the treatment of collateral.

Umbrella supervision—The term applied to comprehensive regulation of a holding company and its parts by one or more holding company regulator(s).

Undercapitalized—A condition in which a business does not have enough capital to meet its needs, or to meet its capital requirements if it is a regulated entity.

Variable Rate Demand Obligation—A security which pays a variable interest rate, and can be redeemed upon the demand of the holder.

Write-Downs—Reducing the value of an asset as it is carried on a firm's balance sheet because the market value has fallen.

APPENDIX B. ACRONYMS

Acronym	Name
AIG	American International Group, Inc.
ASC	Accounting Standards Codification released by the FASB
BAB	Build America Bonds
BHC	Bank Holding Company
BIS	Bank for International Settlements
CDS	Credit Default Swap
CFTC	Commodity Futures Trading Commission
CPP	Capital Purchase Program
DFA	The Dodd-Frank Act: P.L. 111-203
ETF	Exchange Traded Fund
FASB	Financial Accounting Standards Board
FDIC	Federal Deposit Insurance Corporation

Acronym	Name
FFIEC	Federal Financial Institution Examination Council
FHA	Federal Housing Administration
FHC	Financial Holding Company
FHFA	Federal Housing Finance Agency
FRB or the Fed	Federal Reserve Board of Governors
FRBNY	Federal Reserve Bank of New York
FSOC	Financial Stability Oversight Council
FTE	Full-Time Employee Equivalent
GDP	Gross Domestic Product
GSE	Government-Sponsored Enterprise
HUD	Department of Housing and Urban Development
LCBO	Large, Complex Banking Organization
MMF	Money Market Fund
NAV	Net Asset Value
NCUA	National Credit Union Administration
OCC	Office of the Comptroller of the Currency
OFR	Office of Financial Research
OTS	Office of Thrift Supervision
QM	Qualified Mortgage
QRM	Qualified Residential Mortgage
SEC	Securities and Exchange Commission
SIPC	Securities Investor Protection Corporation
TBTF	Too Big To Fail
VRDO	Variable Rate Demand Obligations

End Notes

[1] For more information, see CRS Report RL34427, Financial Turmoil: Federal Reserve Policy Responses, by Marc Labonte.

[2] Prudential regulation under the SEC's Consolidated Supervised Entities program was voluntarily accepted by some U.S. non-depositories in response to proposals by European bank regulators to regulate U.S. firms that did not have comparable prudential regulation. A senior advisor to the SEC testified to the FCIC that he believed that the SEC had sufficient legal authority to regulate Bear Stearns's leverage ratio and balance sheet. Financial Crisis Inquiry Commission, The Financial Crisis Inquiry Report, Washington, DC, January 2011, p. 283, http://www.gpoaccess.gov/ fcic/fcic.pdf.

[3] Donald L Kohn, "The Federal Reserve's Policy Actions during the Financial Crisis and Lessons for the Future," Speech, Carleton University, Ottawa, Canada, Board of Governors of the

Federal Reserve System, 13 May 2010, available at http://www.federalreserve.gov/newsevents/speech/kohn20100513a.htm.

[4] Ibid.

[5] A qualified financial contract is a term of art for certain financial contracts, including derivatives, that are executed and netted immediately upon declaration of bankruptcy. Therefore, uncertainty is probably not the primary concern for these particular financial contracts.

[6] Unemployment statistics are available through the Bureau of Labor Statistics at http://www.bls.gov. Information on the value of total output is available through the Bureau of Economic Analysis, at http://www.bea.gov.

[7] Financial Stability Oversight Council, Annual Report, Washington, DC, July 26, 2011, p. 3, available at http://www.treasury.gov/initiatives/fsoc/Pages/annual-report.aspx.

[8] Ibid., p.131.

[9] Ibid., p.132.

[10] Governor Daniel K. Tarullo, "Regulating Systemic Risk," Speech, 2011 Credit Markets Symposium, North Carolina, Charlotte, March 31, 2011, Board of Governors of the Federal Reserve System, available at http://www.federalreserve.gov/newsevents/ speech/tarullo 20110331a.htm.

[11] Historically, canaries were used as sentinels to test air quality in poorly ventilated underground mines because they are more sensitive to certain odorless, toxic, or explosive gases.

[12] P.L. 111-203 §111(e).

[13] P.L. 111-203 §113(c) authorizes the FSOC to designate as systemically important a firm that has organized itself in such a way as to avoid such designation.

[14] P.L. 111-203 §117.

[15] P.L. 111-203 §123.

[16] P.L. 111-203 §203(b).

[17] P.L. 111-203 §203(D).

[18] Further, the Secretary may invest unused portions of the fund for receivership in obligations of the United States, and the Secretary may purchase obligations for the FDIC to proceed in its receivership powers. The Secretary determines the interest based upon yields on U.S. debt plus a surcharge based upon the spread between U.S. securities and corporate bonds of comparable maturity. These transactions may be considered U.S. public debt, and proceeds from sales reduce the public debt. The Secretary jointly consults with the FDIC in determining the rules and regulations for the maximum obligations that can be used in relation to the assets of a failing firm subject to FDIC resolution.

[19] P.L. 111-203 §203-4.

[20] P.L. 111-203 §210(n)(9)(A).

[21] "FRB: Mission," Board of Governors of the Federal Reserve System, available at http://www.federalreserve.gov/ aboutthefed/mission.htm.

[22] For an in depth review in this area, see CRS Report R41384, The Dodd-Frank Wall Street Reform and Consumer Protection Act: Systemic Risk and the Federal Reserve, by Marc Labonte.

[23] P.L. 111-203 §121.

[24] P.L. 111-203 §161.

[25] P.L. 111-203 §165.

[26] For an in-depth review in this area, see CRS Report R40530, Insolvency of Systemically Significant Financial Companies (SSFCs): Bankruptcy vs. Conservatorship/Receivership, by David H. Carpenter.

[27] As noted above however, the SEC evaluates the likelihood of default for broker-dealers, and the Director of the Federal Insurance Office evaluates insurance firms.

[28] P.L. 111-203 §203(a)(2).

[29] 2013 Annual Report, Financial Stability Oversight Council, available at http://www.treasury.gov/initiatives/fsoc/ Documents/FSOC%202013%20Annual%20Report.pdf.

30 Ibid., p. 64.

[31] Ibid., p. 3.

[32] Ibid., p. 135.

[33] Ibid., p. 137.

[34] Ibid., p. 30.

[35] Ibid., p. 8.

[36] Ibid., p. 144.

[37] Ibid., p. 8.

In: Asset Management ...
Editor: Leah T. McLain
ISBN: 978-1-63117-722-4

Chapter 3

MONITORING THE FINANCIAL SYSTEM[*]

Ben S. Bernanke

We are now more than four years beyond the most intense phase of the financial crisis, but its legacy remains. Our economy has not yet fully regained the jobs lost in the recession that accompanied the financial near collapse. And our financial system-- despite significant healing over the past four years-- continues to struggle with the economic, legal, and reputational consequences of the events of 2007 to 2009.

The crisis also engendered major shifts in financial regulatory policy and practice. Not since the Great Depression have we seen such extensive changes in financial regulation as those codified in the Dodd-Frank Wall Street Reform and Consumer Protection Act (Dodd-Frank Act) in the United States and, internationally, in the Basel III Accord and a range of other initiatives. This new regulatory framework is still under construction, but the Federal Reserve has already made significant changes to how it conceptualizes and carries out both its regulatory and supervisory role and its responsibility to foster financial stability.

In my remarks today I will discuss the Federal Reserve's efforts in an area that typically gets less attention than the writing and implementation of new rules--namely, our ongoing monitoring of the financial system. Of course, the Fed has always paid close attention to financial markets, for both regulatory

[*] This is an edited, reformatted and augmented version of a speech by the Chairman of the Federal Reserve Board, presented at the 49th Annual Conference on Bank Structure and Competition sponsored by the Federal Reserve Bank of Chicago, May 10, 2013.

and monetary policy purposes. However, in recent years, we have both greatly increased the resources we devote to monitoring and taken a more systematic and intensive approach, led by our Office of Financial Stability Policy and Research and drawing on substantial resources from across the Federal Reserve System. This monitoring informs the policy decisions of both the Federal Reserve Board and the Federal Open Market Committee as well as our work with other agencies.

The step-up in our monitoring is motivated importantly by a shift in financial regulation and supervision toward a more macroprudential, or systemic, approach, supplementing our traditional microprudential perspective focused primarily on the health of individual institutions and markets. In the spirit of this more systemic approach to oversight, the Dodd-Frank Act created the Financial Stability Oversight Council (FSOC), which is comprised of the heads of a number of federal and state regulatory agencies. The FSOC has fostered greater interaction among financial regulatory agencies as well as a sense of common responsibility for overall financial stability. Council members regularly discuss risks to financial stability and produce an annual report, which reviews potential risks and recommends ways to mitigate them.[1] The Federal Reserve's broad-based monitoring efforts have been essential for promoting a close and well-informed collaboration with other FSOC members.

A Focus on Vulnerabilities

Ongoing monitoring of the financial system is vital to the macroprudential approach to regulation. Systemic risks can only be defused if they are first identified. That said, it is reasonable to ask whether systemic risks can in fact be reliably identified in advance; after all, neither the Federal Reserve nor economists in general predicted the past crisis. To respond to this point, I will distinguish, as I have elsewhere, between triggers and vulnerabilities.[2] The *triggers* of any crisis are the particular events that touch off the crisis--the proximate causes, if you will. For the 2007-09 crisis, a prominent trigger was the losses suffered by holders of subprime mortgages. In contrast, the *vulnerabilities* associated with a crisis are preexisting features of the financial system that amplify and propagate the initial shocks. Examples of vulnerabilities include high levels of leverage, maturity transformation, interconnectedness, and complexity, all of which have the potential to magnify shocks to the financial system. Absent vulnerabilities, triggers might produce sizable losses to certain firms, investors, or asset classes but would generally not lead to full-blown financial crises; the collapse of the relatively small market for subprime mortgages, for example, would not have been nearly as consequential without preexisting fragilities in securitization practices and short-term funding markets which greatly increased its impact. Of course, monitoring can and does attempt to identify potential triggers--indications of an asset bubble, for example--but shocks of one kind or another are inevitable, so identifying and addressing vulnerabilities is key to ensuring that the financial system overall is robust. Moreover, attempts to address specific vulnerabilities can be supplemented by broader measures--such as requiring banks to hold more capital and liquidity--that make the system more resilient to a range of shocks.

Two other related points motivate our increased monitoring. The first is that the financial system is dynamic and evolving not only because of innovation and the changing needs of the economy, but also because financial activities tend to migrate from more-regulated to less-regulated sectors. An innovative feature of the Dodd-Frank Act is that it includes mechanisms to permit the regulatory system, at least in some circumstances, to adapt to such changes. For example, the act gives the FSOC powers to designate systemically important institutions, market utilities, and activities for additional oversight. Such designation is essentially a determination that an institution or activity creates or exacerbates a vulnerability of the financial system, a determination that can only be made with comprehensive monitoring and analysis.

The second motivation for more intensive monitoring is the apparent tendency for financial market participants to take greater risks when macro conditions are relatively stable. Indeed, it may be that prolonged economic stability is a double-edged sword. To be sure, a favorable overall environment reduces credit risk and strengthens balance sheets, all else being equal, but it could also reduce the incentives for market participants to take reasonable precautions, which may lead in turn to a buildup of financial vulnerabilities. Probably our best defense against complacency during extended periods of calm is careful monitoring for signs of emerging vulnerabilities and, where appropriate, the development of macroprudential and other policy tools that can be used to address them.

The Federal Reserve' s Financial Stability Monitoring Program

So, what specifically does the Federal Reserve monitor? In the remainder of my remarks, I'll highlight and discuss four components of the financial system that are among those we follow most closely: systemically important financial institutions (SIFIs), shadow banking, asset markets, and the nonfinancial sector.[3]

Systemically Important Financial Institutions

SIFIs are financial firms whose distress or failure has the potential to create broader financial instability sufficient to inflict meaningful damage on the real economy. SIFIs tend to be large, but size is not the only factor used to determine whether a firm is systemically important; other factors include the firm's interconnectedness with the rest of the financial system, the complexity and opacity of its operations, the nature and extent of its risk-taking, its use of leverage, its reliance on short-term wholesale funding, and the extent of its cross-border operations. Under the Dodd-Frank Act, the largest bank holding companies are treated as SIFIs; in addition, as I mentioned, the act gives the FSOC the power to designate individual nonbank financial companies as systemically important. This designation process is under way.

Dodd-Frank also establishes a framework for subjecting SIFIs to comprehensive supervisory oversight and enhanced prudential standards. For all such companies, the Federal Reserve will have access to confidential supervisory information and will monitor standard indicators such as regulatory capital, leverage, and funding mix. However, some of these measures, such as regulatory capital ratios, tend to be backward looking and thus may be slow to flag unexpected, rapid changes in the condition of a firm. Accordingly, we supplement the more standard measures with other types of information.

One valuable source of supplementary information is stress testing. Regular, comprehensive stress tests are an increasingly important component of the Federal Reserve's supervisory toolkit, having been used in our assessment of large bank holding companies since 2009.[4] To administer a stress test, supervisors first construct a hypothetical scenario that assumes a set of highly adverse economic and financial developments--for example, a deep recession combined with sharp declines in the prices of houses and other assets. The tested firms and their supervisors then independently estimate firms' projected losses, revenues, and capital under the hypothetical scenario, and the results are publicly disclosed. Firms are evaluated both on their post-stress capital levels and on their ability to analyze their exposures and capital needs.

Stress testing provides a number of advantages over more-standard approaches to assessing capital adequacy. First, measures of capital based on stress tests are both more forward looking and more robust to "tail risk"--that is, to extremely adverse developments of the sort most likely to foster broad-based financial instability. Second, because the Federal Reserve conducts stress tests simultaneously on the major institutions it supervises, the results can be used both for comparative analyses across firms and to judge the collective susceptibility of major financial institutions to certain types of shocks. Indeed, comparative reviews of large financial institutions have become an increasingly important part of the Federal Reserve's supervisory toolkit more generally. Third, the disclosure of stress-test results, which increased investor confidence during the crisis, can also strengthen market discipline in normal times. The stress tests thus provide critical information about key financial institutions while also forcing the firms to improve their ability to measure and manage their risk exposures.

Stress-testing techniques can also be used in more-focused assessments of the banking sector's vulnerability to specific risks not captured in the main scenario, such as liquidity risk or interest rate risk. Like comprehensive stress tests, such focused exercises are an important element of our supervision of SIFIs. For example, supervisors are collecting detailed data on liquidity that help them compare firms' susceptibilities to various types of funding stresses and to evaluate firms' strategies for managing their liquidity. Supervisors also are working with firms to assess how profitability and capital would fare under various stressful interest rate scenarios.

Federal Reserve staff members supplement supervisory and stress-test information with other measures. For example, though supervisors have long appreciated the value of market-based indicators in evaluating the conditions of systemically important firms (or, indeed, any publicly traded firm), our monitoring program uses market information to a much greater degree than in the past. Thus, in addition to standard indicators--such as stock prices and the prices of credit default swaps, which capture market views about individual firms--we use market-based measures of systemic stability derived from recent research. These measures use correlations of asset prices to capture the market's perception of a given firm's potential to destabilize the financial system at a time when the broader financial markets are stressed; other measures estimate the vulnerability of a given firm to disturbances emanating from elsewhere in the system.[5] The further development of market-based measures of systemic vulnerabilities and systemic risk is a lively area of research.

Network analysis, yet another promising tool under active development, has the potential to help us better monitor the interconnectedness of financial institutions and markets. Interconnectedness can arise from common holdings of assets or through the exposures of firms to their counterparties. Network measures rely on concepts used in engineering, communications, and neuroscience to map linkages among financial firms and market activities. The goals are to identify key nodes or clusters that could destabilize the system and to simulate how a shock, such as the sudden distress of a firm, could be transmitted and amplified through the network. These tools can also be used to analyze the systemic stability effects of a change in the structure of a network. For example, margin rules affect the sensitivity of firms to the conditions of their counterparties; thus, margin rules affect the likelihood of financial contagion through various firms and markets.

Shadow Banking

Shadow banking, a second area we closely monitor, was an important source of instability during the crisis. Shadow banking comprises various markets and institutions that provide financial intermediation outside the traditional, regulated banking system. Shadow banking includes vehicles for credit intermediation, maturity transformation, liquidity provision, and risk sharing. Such vehicles are typically funded on a largely short-term basis from wholesale sources. In the run-up to the crisis, the shadow banking sector involved a high degree of maturity transformation and leverage. Illiquid loans to households and businesses were securitized, and the tranches of the securitizations with the highest credit ratings were funded by very short-term debt, such as asset-backed commercial paper and repurchase agreements (repos). The short-term funding was in turn provided by institutions, such as money market funds, whose investors expected payment in full on demand and had little tolerance for risk to principal.

As it turned out, the ultimate investors did not fully understand the quality of the assets they were financing. Investors were lulled by triple-A credit ratings and by expected support from sponsoring institutions--support that was, in fact, discretionary and not always provided. When investors lost confidence in the quality of the assets or in the institutions expected to provide support, they ran. Their flight created serious funding pressures throughout the financial system, threatened the solvency of many firms, and inflicted serious damage on the broader economy.

Securities broker-dealers play a central role in many aspects of shadow banking as facilitators of market-based intermediation. To finance their own and their clients' securities holdings, broker-dealers tend to rely on short-term collateralized funding, often in the form of repo agreements with highly risk-averse lenders. The crisis revealed that this funding is potentially quite fragile if lenders have limited capacity to analyze the collateral or counterparty risks associated with short-term secured lending, but rather look at these transactions as nearly risk free. As questions emerged about the nature and value of collateral, worried lenders either greatly increased margin requirements or, more commonly, pulled back entirely. Borrowers unable to meet margin calls and finance their asset holdings were forced to sell, driving down asset prices further and setting off a cycle of deleveraging and further asset liquidation.

To monitor intermediation by broker-dealers, the Federal Reserve in 2010 created a quarterly Senior Credit Officer Opinion Survey on Dealer Financing Terms, which asks dealers about the credit they provide.[6] Modeled on the long-established Senior Loan Officer Opinion Survey on Bank Lending Practices sent to commercial banks, the survey of senior credit officers at dealers tracks conditions in markets such as those for securities financing, prime brokerage, and derivatives trading.[7] The credit officer survey is designed to monitor potential vulnerabilities stemming from the greater use of leverage by investors (particularly through lending backed by less-liquid collateral) or increased volumes of maturity transformation. Before the financial crisis, we had only very limited information regarding such trends.

We have other potential sources of information about shadow banking. The Treasury Department's Office of Financial Research and Federal Reserve staff are collaborating to construct data sets on triparty and bilateral repo transactions, which should facilitate the development of better monitoring metrics for repo activity and improve transparency in these markets. We also talk regularly to market participants about developments, paying particular attention to the creation of new financial vehicles that foster greater maturity transformation outside the regulated sector, provide funding for less-liquid assets, or transform risks from forms that are more easily measured to forms that are more opaque.

A fair summary is that, while the shadow banking sector is smaller today than before the crisis and some of its least stable components have either disappeared or been reformed, regulators and the private sector need to address remaining vulnerabilities. For example, although money market funds were strengthened by reforms undertaken by the Securities and Exchange Commission (SEC) in 2010, the possibility of a run on these funds remains--for instance, if a fund should "break the buck," or report a net asset value below 99.5 cents, as the Reserve Primary Fund did in 2008. The risk is increased by the fact that the Treasury no longer has the power to guarantee investors' holdings in money funds, an authority that was critical for stopping the 2008 run. In November 2012, the FSOC proposed for public comment some alternative approaches for the reform of money funds. The SEC is currently considering these and other possible steps.

With respect to the triparty repo platform, progress has been made in reducing the amount of intraday credit extended by the clearing banks in the course of the daily settlement process, and, as additional enhancements are made, the extension of such credit should be largely eliminated by the end of 2014. However, important risks remain in the short-term wholesale funding markets. One of the key risks is how the system would respond to the failure of a broker-dealer or other major borrower. The Dodd-Frank Act has provided important additional tools to deal with this vulnerability, notably the provisions that facilitate an orderly resolution of a broker-dealer or a broker-dealer holding company whose imminent failure poses a systemic risk. But, as highlighted in the FSOC's most recent annual report, more work is needed to better prepare investors and other market participants to deal with the potential consequences of a default by a large participant in the repo market.[8]

Asset Markets

Asset markets are a third area that we closely monitor. We follow developments in markets for a wide range of assets, including public and private fixed-income instruments, corporate equities, real estate, commodities, and structured credit products, among others. Foreign as well as domestic markets receive close attention, as do global linkages, such as the effects of the ongoing European fiscal and banking problems on U.S. markets.

Not surprisingly, we try to identify unusual patterns in valuations, such as historically high or low ratios of prices to earnings in equity markets. We use a variety of models and methods; for example, we use empirical models of default risk and risk premiums to analyze credit spreads in corporate bond markets. These assessments are complemented by other information, including measures of volumes, liquidity, and market functioning, as well as intelligence gleaned from market participants and outside analysts. In light of the current low interest rate environment, we are watching particularly closely for instances of "reaching for yield" and other forms of excessive risk-taking, which may affect asset prices and their relationships with fundamentals. It is worth emphasizing that looking for historically unusual patterns or relationships in asset prices can be useful even if you believe that asset markets are generally efficient in setting prices. For the purpose of safeguarding financial stability, we are less concerned about whether a given asset price is justified in some average sense than in the possibility of a sharp move. Asset prices that are far from historically normal levels would seem to be more susceptible to such destabilizing moves.

From a financial stability perspective, however, the assessment of asset valuations is only the first step of the analysis. Also to be considered are factors such as the leverage and degree of maturity mismatch being used by the holders of the asset, the liquidity of the asset, and the sensitivity of the asset's value to changes in broad financial conditions. Differences in these factors help explain why the correction in equity markets in 2000 and 2001 did not induce widespread systemic disruptions, while the collapse in house prices and in the quality of mortgage credit during the 2007-09 crisis had much more far-reaching effects: The losses from the stock market declines in 2000 and 2001 were widely diffused, while mortgage losses were concentrated--and, through various financial instruments, amplified--in critical parts of the financial system, resulting ultimately in panic, asset fire sales, and the collapse of credit markets.

Nonfinancial Sector

Our financial stability monitoring extends to the nonfinancial sector, including households and businesses. Research has identified excessive growth in credit and leverage in the private nonfinancial sector as potential indicators of systemic risk.[9] Highly leveraged or financially fragile households and businesses are less able to withstand adverse changes in income or wealth, including those brought about by deteriorating conditions in financial and credit markets. A highly leveraged economy is also more prone to so-called financial accelerator effects, as when financially stressed firms are forced to lay off workers who, in turn, lacking financial reserves, sharply cut their own spending. Financial stress in the nonfinancial sector--for example, higher default rates on mortgages or corporate debt--can also damage financial institutions, creating a potential adverse feedback loop as they reduce the availability of credit and shed assets to conserve capital, thereby further weakening the financial positions of households and firms.

The vulnerabilities of the nonfinancial sector can potentially be captured by both stock measures (such as wealth and leverage) and flow measures (such as the ratio of debt service to income). Sector-wide data are available from a number of sources, importantly the Federal Reserve's flow of funds accounts, which is a set of aggregate integrated financial accounts that measures sources and uses of funds for major sectors as well as for the economy as a whole.[10] These accounts allow us to trace the flow of credit from its sources, such as banks or wholesale funding markets, to the household and business sectors that receive it.

The Federal Reserve also now monitors detailed consumer- and business-level data suited for picking up changes in the nature of borrowing and lending, as well as for tracking financial conditions of those most exposed to a cyclical downturn or a reversal of fortunes. For example, during the housing boom, the aggregate data accurately showed the outsized pace of home mortgage borrowing, but it could not reveal the pervasive deterioration in underwriting that implied a substantial increase in the underlying credit risk from that activity.[11] More recently, gains in household net worth have been concentrated among wealthier households, while many households in the middle or lower parts of the distribution have experienced declines in wealth since the crisis. Moreover, many homeowners remain "underwater," with their homes worth less than the principal balances on their mortgages. Thus, more detailed information clarifies that many households remain more financially fragile than might be inferred from the aggregate statistics alone.

CONCLUSION

In closing, let me reiterate that while the effective regulation and supervision of individual financial institutions will always be crucial to ensuring a well-functioning financial system, the Federal Reserve is moving toward a more systemic approach that also pays close attention to the vulnerabilities of the financial system as a whole. Toward that end, we are pursuing an active program of financial monitoring, supported by expanded research and data collection, often undertaken in conjunction with other U.S. financial regulatory agencies. Our stepped-up monitoring and analysis is already providing important information for the Board and the Federal Open Market Committee as well as for the broader regulatory community. We will continue to work toward improving our ability to detect and address vulnerabilities in our financial system.

End Notes

[1] For the most recent report, see U.S. Department of the Treasury, Financial Stability Oversight Council (2013), 2013 Annual Report (Washington: Department of the Treasury), www.treasury.gov/initiatives/fsoc/studies-reports/Pages/2013-Annual-Report.aspx.

[2] See Ben S. Bernanke (2010), "Causes of the Recent Financial and Economic Crisis," testimony before the Financial Crisis Inquiry Commission, Washington, September 2, www.federalreserve.gov/newsevents/testimony/bernanke20100902a.htm; and Ben S. Bernanke (2012), "Some Reflections on the Crisis and the Policy Response," speech delivered at "Rethinking Finance: Perspectives on the Crisis," a conference sponsored by the Russell Sage Foundation and The Century Foundation, New York, April 13, www.federal reserve.gov/newsevents/speech/bernanke20120413a.htm.

[3] The remainder of my remarks draws heavily on Tobias Adrian, Daniel Covitz, and Nellie Liang (2013), "Financial Stability Monitoring," Finance and Economics Discussion Series 2013-21 (Washington: Board of Governors of the Federal Reserve System, April), www.federalreserve.gov/pubs/feds/2013/201321/201321pap.pdf. This paper provides more details on the Federal Reserve's financial stability monitoring program. I thank the authors for their assistance with these remarks.

[4] The Federal Reserve's stress-testing program is discussed in Ben S. Bernanke (2013), "Stress Testing Banks: What Have We Learned?" speech delivered at "Maintaining Financial Stability: Holding a Tiger by the Tail," a financial markets conference sponsored by the Federal Reserve Bank of Atlanta, held in Stone Mountain, Ga., April 8-10, www.federal reserve.gov/newsevents/speech/bernanke20130408a.htm. More limited forms of stress testing were used by supervisors before 2009.

[5] For example, conditional value at risk provides an estimate of the systemic importance of a firm at a moment in time, based on how the firm's equity value and broader equity values co-vary when overall conditions are very adverse; see Tobias Adrian and Markus K. Brunnermeier (2008; revised September 2011), "CoVaR," Staff Reports 348 (New York: Federal Reserve Bank of New York, September), www.newyorkfed.org/ research/ staff_reports/sr348.pdf. The distressed insurance premium uses information from firms' credit default swap spreads and equity prices to measure the implied cost of insuring a given firm against broader financial distress--an indicator of the vulnerability of the firm to systemic instability; see Xin Huang, Hao Zhou, and Haibin Zhu (2009), "A Framework for Assessing the Systemic Risk of Major Financial Institutions," Journal of Banking and Finance, vol. 33 (November), pp. 2036-49. The systemic expected shortfall uses firm equity prices, leverage, and volatility to measure the propensity of a firm to be undercapitalized given a marketwide decline in equity prices; see Viral V. Acharya, Lasse H. Pedersen, Thomas Philippon, and Matthew Richardson (2010), "Measuring Systemic Risk," unpublished paper, New York University, Leonard Stern School of Business, May, http://vlab.stern.nyu.edu/public/static/SR-v3.pdf.

[6] The Senior Credit Officer Opinion Survey on Dealer Financing Terms is available on the Federal Reserve Board's website at www.federalreserve.gov/econresdata /releases/ scoos.htm.

[7] The Senior Loan Officer Opinion Survey on Bank Lending Practices is available on the Federal Reserve Board's website at www.federalreserve.gov/boarddocs/SnLoanSurvey/default.htm.

[8] See Financial Stability Oversight Council, 2013 Annual Report, in note 1.

[9] See, for example, Mathias Drehmann, Claudio Borio, and Kostas Tsatsaronis (2011), "Anchoring Countercyclical Capital Buffers: The Role of Credit Aggregates," International Journal of Central Banking, vol. 7 (December), pp. 189-240; and Rochelle M. Edge and Ralf R. Meisenzahl (2011), "The Unreliability of Credit-to-GDP Ratio Gaps in Real Time: Implications for Countercyclical Capital Buffers," International Journal of Central Banking, vol. 7 (December), pp. 261-98.

[10] The flow of funds data are available on the Federal Reserve Board's website at www.federalreserve.gov/releases/z1.

[11] See Matthew J. Eichner, Donald L. Kohn, and Michael G. Palumbo (2010), "Financial Statistics for the United States and the Crisis: What Did They Get Right, What Did They Miss, and How Should They Change?" Finance and Economics Discussion Series 2010-20 (Washington: Board of Governors of the Federal Reserve System, April), www.federalreserve.gov/pubs/feds/2010/201020/201020pap.pdf.

INDEX

A

accelerator, 87
access, 12, 47, 58, 60, 71, 82
accounting, 19, 26, 54, 72
agencies, 44, 45, 49, 52, 53, 59, 70, 72, 80
aggregate demand, 61
air quality, 76
arbitrage, 19, 39
Asia, 38
assessment, 82, 87
asset management firms, vii, 1, 2, 3, 4, 29
assets, 1, 2, 3, 4, 5, 6, 10, 11, 12, 14, 15, 17, 19, 20, 21, 23, 25, 27, 28, 29, 30, 31, 34, 39, 40, 41, 42, 46, 47, 48, 51, 52, 56, 57, 65, 69, 70, 71, 72, 73, 76, 82, 84, 86, 87
authorities, 25
authority, 52, 55, 56, 73, 75, 86

B

backlash, 62
bail, 71, 72
balance sheet, 6, 24, 25, 33, 42, 74, 75, 81
bank charter, 47
bank debt, 21
bank holding companies, 25, 33, 53, 55, 65, 82
Bank of England, 18, 35
bankers, 68
banking, vii, 13, 34, 40, 43, 64, 65, 66, 68, 69, 70, 73, 82, 83, 84, 85, 86
banking sector, 83, 84, 85
bankruptcy, 44, 46, 47, 48, 49, 51, 56, 64, 67, 73, 76
banks, 2, 3, 25, 26, 29, 34, 41, 46, 47, 48, 49, 52, 55, 56, 57, 58, 60, 61, 62, 65, 67, 68, 69, 70, 81, 86, 88
barriers, 27
barriers to entry, 27
BBB, 24
behaviors, 3, 10, 12, 14
benchmarks, 44, 62
benefits, 29, 41, 50, 61
BHC, 74
bond market, 61, 62, 63, 86
bondholders, 71
bonds, 13, 40, 61, 62, 63, 66, 67, 69, 70, 71, 76
borrowers, 19, 20, 58, 59, 62
building blocks, 4
Bureau of Labor Statistics, 76
business model, vii, 4
businesses, 4, 16, 23, 25, 33, 34, 65, 70, 71, 84, 87
buyer, 73
buyers, 22, 62, 68, 71

C

capital adequacy, 82
capital flight, 63
capital markets, 13, 15, 60
Capital Purchase Program, 53, 66, 74
cash, 2, 3, 12, 13, 14, 15, 17, 19, 21, 31, 39, 40, 41, 68, 71, 73
cash flow, 71, 73
central bank, 50, 61, 62, 63, 64
certificates of deposit, 71
challenges, 15
Chicago, vii, 35, 79
classes, 5, 10, 27, 30, 62, 64, 71, 80
clientele, vii, 4
clients, vii, 2, 4, 11, 19, 23, 25, 26, 30, 31, 33, 34, 84
climate, 10
clone, 30
clusters, 84
coal, 51
collaboration, 1, 80
collateral, 2, 3, 12, 17, 19, 27, 31, 32, 49, 51, 58, 68, 72, 74, 85
collateral damage, 49
commercial, 2, 22, 57, 58, 66, 67, 68, 71, 72, 73, 84, 85
commercial bank, 2, 57, 66, 68, 73, 85
commodity, 21, 23, 66, 68, 71
communication, 44, 45, 46, 60
communities, 67
community, 88
competitors, 51, 60, 70
complexity, 22, 23, 51, 80, 82
compliance, 5
composition, 31, 50
computing, 70
conference, 89
Congress, vii, 22, 43, 45, 48, 49, 53, 54, 55, 57
construction, 6, 79
consulting, 23
consumer protection, 59
consumers, 44, 46
coordination, 46
correlations, 23, 83
cost, 4, 12, 54, 61, 89
counseling, 70
CPP, 74
credit market, 71, 87
credit rating, 32, 67, 84
creditors, 25, 27, 48, 51, 54, 57
crises, 64, 80
currency, 40, 63, 68
customers, 33, 41, 66, 72
cyber-attack, 44
cycles, 12
Cyprus, 63, 64, 65

D

danger, 44, 46, 51
data availability, 3
data collection, 29, 88
data set, 85
debt service, 87
debts, 64
deficiencies, 53
deficiency, 19, 56
deflation, 65
Department of Labor, 30
Department of the Treasury, 45, 65, 88
depository institutions, 47, 67, 68, 73
deposits, 2, 39, 47, 48, 49, 57, 58, 61, 65, 67, 68, 69, 71
depreciation, 65
depression, 27
depth, 76
derivatives, 2, 5, 10, 17, 20, 21, 22, 23, 26, 27, 41, 67, 70, 71, 73, 76, 85
devaluation, 64
directives, 55
directors, 52, 57
disclosure, 41, 83
dislocation, 28
distress, 10, 25, 27, 48, 58, 82, 84
distribution, 88
diversification, 41
diversity, vii, 2, 4
domestic markets, 86

drawing, 80
drying, 31

E

earnings, 67, 86
economic leverage, 21
economies of scale, 25
emergency, 41, 58
employees, 5, 23, 39
employment, 55, 67
engineering, 84
environment, 14, 60, 61, 81, 86
equality, 55
equities, 4, 15, 39, 86
equity, 3, 4, 5, 13, 34, 36, 40, 65, 71, 86, 87, 89
equity market, 13, 36, 86, 87
Europe, 22, 64
European Central Bank, 64
evidence, 29
examinations, 30, 41, 56
exchange rate, 64
execution, 14
expenditures, 15
expertise, 45
exports, 64
exposure, 13, 16, 21, 22, 41, 44, 55, 58, 60, 64
externalities, 50

F

Facebook, 60
facilitators, 84
Fannie Mae, 47, 48, 59
FDIC, 35, 44, 45, 46, 47, 49, 52, 54, 55, 56, 57, 74, 76
fear, 19, 58
federal government, 68, 73
Federal Housing Finance Agency(FHFA), 45, 47, 75
federal law, 67, 72
Federal Register, 36, 37, 38
Federal Reserve, vii, 8, 35, 37, 44, 45, 46, 47, 51, 55, 59, 65, 68, 69, 75, 76, 79, 80, 81, 82, 83, 85, 88, 89, 90
Federal Reserve Board, vii, 44, 45, 75, 79, 80, 89, 90
FHFA, 47, 75
fiduciary agents, vii, 4
financial condition, 32, 57, 62, 87, 88
financial crisis, 15, 18, 19, 22, 40, 44, 45, 47, 64, 79, 85
financial data, 44, 72
financial development, 82
financial distress, 19, 69, 89
financial firms, 42, 47, 49, 55, 66, 82, 84
financial instability, 45, 52, 56, 58, 59, 61, 63, 64, 82, 83
financial institutions, vii, 2, 4, 25, 27, 39, 44, 45, 46, 47, 48, 49, 50, 57, 60, 61, 64, 66, 69, 74, 82, 83, 84, 87, 88
financial intermediaries, 44, 58
financial markets, 1, 2, 4, 23, 26, 29, 47, 79, 83, 89
financial regulation, 44, 46, 79, 80
financial reports, 3
Financial Services Authority, 36
financial shocks, 1, 10, 12
financial stability, vii, 1, 2, 12, 17, 23, 29, 30, 31, 32, 41, 44, 46, 49, 50, 51, 54, 55, 57, 59, 62, 63, 64, 69, 79, 80, 86, 87, 89
financial support, 19, 48, 49
financial system, 2, 10, 22, 23, 25, 31, 43, 45, 46, 48, 49, 50, 57, 60, 61, 64, 69, 71, 73, 74, 79, 80, 81, 82, 83, 84, 87, 88
firm size, 48, 51
fiscal deficit, 63
fiscal policy, 62
flexibility, 4, 11, 39
flight, 11, 84
fluctuations, 21, 62
force, 60
foreign exchange, 68
foreign firms, 53, 55
formation, 2
fraud, 72
Freddie Mac, 47, 48, 59

freezing, 40
FSB, 36, 41
funding, 2, 15, 19, 27, 28, 31, 40, 44, 47, 48, 51, 57, 58, 59, 60, 64, 68, 70, 81, 82, 83, 84, 85, 86, 88
funds, 2, 3, 4, 5, 6, 7, 9, 11, 12, 13, 14, 15, 16, 17, 19, 20, 21, 22, 23, 25, 26, 27, 28, 29, 30, 33, 34, 39, 40, 41, 44, 47, 48, 52, 53, 54, 57, 58, 61, 66, 68, 69, 70, 71, 73, 84, 85, 87, 90

G

GDP, 63, 75, 89
governance, 34
government intervention, 69
government revenues, 62
government spending, 62
governments, 51, 63, 64, 71
Gramm-Leach-Bliley Act, 65, 69, 70
grants, 52
Great Depression, 79
Greece, 63, 64
Gross Domestic Product, 75
growth, 4, 13, 63, 65, 87
GSEs, 44, 47, 48, 59, 60, 70
guidelines, 5, 14, 30

H

healing, 79
health, 80
hedging, 19, 70
holding company, 8, 26, 65, 69, 70, 74, 86
homeowners, 88
homes, 88
House, 38, 53, 59
House of Representatives, 38
housing, 44, 59, 61, 88
Housing and Urban Development, 75
HUD, 75
human, 60
human activity, 60
hybrid, 17, 39

I

identification, 45
idiosyncratic, 31
IMA, 30
imbalances, 44, 63
imports, 64
improvements, 59, 60
income, 4, 5, 13, 15, 17, 18, 22, 27, 28, 39, 61, 72, 86, 87
income tax, 72
individuals, 2, 21, 34, 67, 71
industry, vii, 1, 3, 4, 5, 10, 11, 17, 26, 29, 32, 33, 34, 41, 51
information technology, 44
infrastructure, 50, 60
institutions, 2, 4, 27, 38, 39, 46, 47, 48, 49, 54, 62, 64, 66, 68, 69, 72, 73, 80, 81, 82, 83, 84
intelligence, 86
interest rates, 13, 17, 21, 40, 44, 61, 62, 63, 64, 69, 70
intermediaries, 58, 61
international financial institutions, 31
intrinsic value, 14
investment(s), vii, 2, 3, 4, 5, 6, 8, 10, 11, 12, 13, 14, 15, 17, 19, 21, 22, 23, 25, 27, 28, 29, 30, 31, 33, 34, 39, 40, 41, 47, 48, 58, 61, 63, 67, 71, 73
investment bank, 47, 48, 67, 73
investment boutiques, vii, 4
investors, 2, 11, 12, 13, 14, 15, 16, 21, 22, 23, 25, 26, 27, 28, 30, 31, 34, 39, 40, 41, 51, 52, 61, 63, 70, 71, 80, 84, 85, 86
Ireland, 64
isolation, 50
issues, 3, 11, 12, 41, 44, 49, 54, 60, 63, 64
Italy, 64

J

Japan, 65
jurisdiction, 29, 45

L

landscape, 2
laws, 65
lead, 10, 14, 16, 26, 28, 62, 63, 80, 81
lender of last resort, 55, 68
lending, 2, 3, 5, 12, 17, 18, 19, 20, 23, 26, 28, 31, 32, 35, 41, 42, 58, 61, 72, 73, 85, 88
light, 86
liquid assets, 12, 14, 15, 21, 27, 71, 85
liquidate, 25, 72
liquidity, 2, 5, 10, 13, 14, 15, 16, 17, 19, 20, 22, 25, 27, 28, 29, 30, 31, 32, 34, 39, 40, 41, 44, 47, 51, 55, 61, 62, 81, 83, 84, 86, 87
loans, 27, 41, 47, 51, 57, 58, 59, 61, 64, 66, 67, 68, 69, 71, 72, 73, 84

M

macroeconomic policies, 44
macroeconomic policy, 44
macroprudential analysis, 29
magnitude, 25, 45
majority, 13, 53, 54
management, vii, 1, 2, 3, 4, 5, 6, 9, 10, 11, 12, 14, 15, 16, 17, 22, 23, 25, 26, 27, 28, 29, 30, 33, 34, 38, 39, 42, 69
manipulation, 61
market concentration, 32
market discipline, 49, 83
market position, 27
market segment, 10, 13, 14, 23, 32
market share, 59
marketing, 70
marketplace, 68
measurement(s), 32, 72
membership, vii, 43, 52, 67, 72
metals, 68, 70
mission, vii, 43, 46, 49, 50, 55, 76
models, 86
monetary policy, 55, 69, 80
money markets, 19
monopoly, 51
moral hazard, 54, 71
mortgage-backed securities, 17, 22, 59
motivation, 81

N

natural disaster(s), 60
neuroscience, 84
New York Stock Exchange, 60
niche market, 27
nodes, 84

O

officials, 64
opacity, 82
operations, 69, 82
oversight, 29, 33, 80, 81, 82
ownership, 30, 34, 65, 66, 73

P

Pacific, 7, 8
parallel, 3, 73
parity, 5
participants, 2, 13, 26, 27, 28, 32, 33, 39, 50, 51, 62, 81, 85, 86
pension plans, 30
permit, 15, 81
pessimism, 59
platform, 86
policy, vii, 2, 25, 41, 43, 46, 52, 62, 65, 74, 79, 80, 81
policy issues, vii, 43
policy responses, 65
policymakers, 49, 64
pools, 70, 71
population, 2
portfolio, 4, 5, 10, 11, 13, 14, 20, 23, 26, 27
portfolio investment, 26
portfolio management, 4, 23
Portugal, 64
Preferred Stock Purchase Agreements, 59

president, 45, 52
price stability, 55
primary function, 72
private sector, 54, 85
probability, 28
professionals, 50
profit, 68, 73
profitability, 83
project, 62
proliferation, 50
protection, 22, 30, 46, 68, 71, 72
prudential regulation, 41, 44, 46, 47, 75
PSPAs, 59
public debt, 76
public support, 48

R

rating agencies, 26
real estate, 86
recall, 19
recession, 79, 82
recommendations, 43, 49, 53, 55
recovery, 38, 59
reform(s), 3, vii, 36, 38, 43, 45, 49, 62, 76, 79, 85, 86
regulations, 15, 22, 30, 34, 46, 50, 53, 54, 59, 68, 76
regulatory agencies, 80, 88
regulatory framework, 30, 43, 45, 46, 79
reliability, 44, 64
repo, 3, 5, 23, 28, 31, 40, 42, 58, 60, 84, 85, 86
reputation, 16, 23, 28
requirements, 29, 33, 34, 41, 46, 55, 57, 66, 70, 74, 85
resale, 71
researchers, 29
reserves, 17, 25, 41, 87
residential, 75
resilience, 44, 60, 62
resolution, 25, 44, 46, 47, 48, 49, 54, 55, 57, 63, 76, 86
resources, 25, 52, 69, 80
response, 14, 15, 30, 75
restrictions, 11, 15, 21, 30
restructuring, 64
retail, 13, 15, 21, 22, 60
retirement, 33, 34
revenue, 62
rights, 14, 56
risk management, 5, 11, 16, 17, 19, 22, 23, 26, 55
risk-taking, 29, 82, 86
rules, 31, 34, 40, 44, 46, 54, 59, 68, 76, 79, 84

S

safe haven, 63
safety, 46, 61, 68
savings, 61, 66, 67, 68, 72, 74
savings banks, 72
scope, vii, 43, 51, 52
Secretary of the Treasury, 45, 52, 53
securities, vii, 2, 3, 5, 10, 12, 13, 14, 15, 17, 18, 19, 20, 23, 26, 27, 28, 30, 31, 32, 34, 35, 39, 40, 41, 42, 43, 45, 48, 52, 57, 58, 60, 63, 65, 66, 67, 68, 69, 70, 71, 72, 73, 76, 84, 85
Securities Act of 1933, 34
securities firms, 69, 70
security, 5, 19, 40, 60, 65, 68, 71, 73, 74
seed, 25, 39
segregation, 70
seller(s), 22, 58, 68, 71
Senate, 38, 52, 53
sensitivity, 62, 84, 87
service provider, 13, 26
services, vii, 2, 4, 5, 16, 19, 23, 26, 33, 34, 46, 51, 65, 67, 70, 72, 73
settlements, 22
severe stress, 15
shareholders, 30, 40, 57
shock, 10, 13, 14, 17, 28, 30, 61, 84
shortfall, 89
signs, 59, 81
solution, 4
speech, vii, 76, 79, 89
spending, 62, 63, 87

stability, 15, 16, 31, 46, 49, 50, 60, 65, 80, 81, 83, 84
staff members, 83
state(s), 6, 30, 33, 34, 41, 45, 49, 52, 55, 56, 65, 67, 68, 69, 72, 73, 80
statistics, 76, 88
statutes, 65
stock, 19, 21, 29, 59, 60, 68, 83, 87
stock price, 21, 83
storage, 60
stress, 13, 14, 15, 19, 23, 25, 26, 27, 28, 31, 41, 61, 64, 82, 83, 87, 89
stress test, 25, 82, 83, 89
stress testing, 82, 89
structure, 5, 26, 39, 67, 70, 84
style, 4
substitutes, 2, 51
supervision, 1, 23, 46, 53, 55, 67, 74, 80, 83, 88
supervisor(s), 29, 45, 82, 83, 89
susceptibility, 83
suspensions, 15
systemic risk, 43, 46, 49, 50, 51, 52, 53, 54, 55, 56, 57, 60, 69, 73, 80, 83, 86, 87

T

target, 64
tax increase, 63
taxes, 72
teams, 26
techniques, 83
technologies, 2
technology, 60
telecommunications, 60
telephone, 72
telephones, 60
testing, 82, 83, 89
testing program, 89
threats, vii, 1, 10, 23, 28, 49, 57, 62, 64, 69
thrifts, 47, 56, 72
Title I, 50
tracks, 85
trade, 14, 15, 39, 40, 67, 68, 71
tranches, 71, 84
transaction costs, 13
transactions, 3, 5, 19, 21, 28, 31, 34, 39, 51, 52, 64, 66, 72, 76, 85
transformation, 2, 29, 32, 80, 84, 85
transmission, 4, 10
transparency, 31, 52, 85
Treasury, 48, 52, 54, 56, 59, 62, 63, 64, 85
Treasury Secretary, 52, 56
treatment, 74
triggers, 80
trust fund, 33
turbulence, 13, 14, 25

U

U.S. Department of the Treasury, vii, 1, 69, 88
U.S. Treasury, 59, 63, 71
underwriting, 62, 70, 88
unions, 47, 67, 68
United Kingdom, 41
United States, 6, 44, 62, 63, 69, 71, 76, 79, 90

V

valuation, 26, 27, 34
variables, 55
vehicles, 2, 3, 5, 10, 12, 13, 15, 17, 19, 30, 41, 84, 85
veto, 53
volatility, 10, 11, 12, 13, 17, 27, 89
vote, 53, 54, 55
voting, 52
vulnerability, 30, 81, 83, 86, 89

W

Washington, 35, 36, 37, 38, 75, 76, 88, 89, 90
weakness, 23, 29
wealth, 33, 87, 88
websites, 65

wholesale, 40, 44, 57, 58, 59, 60, 82, 84, 86, 88
workers, 87
worldwide, 7

Y

yield, 3, 10, 12, 44, 61, 62, 63, 86